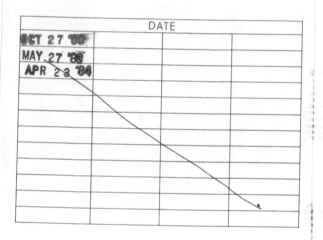

DATE			
OCT 27 '80			
MAY 27 '85			
APR 23 '84			

ANDREW JACKSON

ANDREW JACKSON

*His Contribution to the
American Tradition*

HAROLD C. SYRETT

GREENWOOD PRESS, PUBLISHERS
WESTPORT, CONNECTICUT

To
DOROTHY P. SYRETT AND F. HAROLD SYRETT

GENERAL INTRODUCTION

FOR THE

Makers of the American Tradition Series

THE PURPOSE of this series is to present in a fresh and challenging way the great figures of the American tradition—those individuals who have been most influential throughout the history of the American people in forging that strong and yet complex phenomenon that constitutes what we call the American tradition or the American way of life.

Countless books have been written about these men; a good many books containing their writings and speeches have been published; many biographies of them have appeared. But the *Makers of the American Tradition* Series is a genuinely new approach to the story of our heritage. These books are not biographies; they are not anthologies. They are a combination of original text and interpretation. They embody a new and fresh approach because they combine the best and most characteristic of the original written and recorded spoken words of outstanding American figures with thoughtful and incisive interpretations by the distinguished scholars chosen to put these books together.

In each volume the focus is upon those elements in the contributions of these Americans—whether in terms of original thought or articulate and decisive leadership—

7

which best characterize the *particular* quality, in each case, of the contribution. All other aspects of, say, Benjamin Franklin or Andrew Jackson or Roger Williams are in these books subordinated to what each had most peculiarly to contribute to the shaping of the American tradition.

When we speak of the American tradition, we are, of course, referring to a complex of various and sometimes opposing traditions, but if there is any single outstanding American principle, I suppose that it is that of the finding of unity through multiplicity and diversity. The American tradition, a composite in itself, is analagous to the United States and the American people, each being a complex of many simples.

Similarly, when we speak of the *makers* of this tradition, we are, of course, aware that no ten or twenty or fifty men, however talented, however able, really *made* this tradition. Nevertheless, the individuals we have chosen as the subjects for these books seem to us to have been outstandingly important in shaping the way of life that is our heritage today. Hence, just as we welcome in the American tradition its superficially strange mixture of radical idealism and plain horse sense, of a general love of liberty and a sober sense of social responsibility, of honest conservatism and honest dissidence, so we welcome in this series such conflicting or disparate figures as Thomas Jefferson and Alexander Hamilton, Roger Williams and John C. Calhoun, Cotton Mather and John Dewey.

For whom is this series intended? It is our hope and belief that it is intended for every literate American of whatever age and description. For we are firmly convinced that the books in this series will leave their readers with a far more concise and exact idea of what the great leaders of the American people have thought, said and stood for, than they have ever had before. Much has been made and is being made of the confusion and anxiety under which all of us labor today. Much has been said in various ways of the extent to which all people, and among them notably Americans, are searching for their souls. Much has been said about both the external and internal threats to our American way of life—threats that many Americans, with whatever different interpretations, feel surround us on all sides. We are faced unquestionably with the challenge of building a free and confident America, for ourselves and for the free world in our time.

In a time of crisis, how may we find that strength and that confidence? It seems to me that it is a constant in human nature at such times to turn inward, to return to one's roots, one's origins, to find such resources. I believe this to be as true for peoples as for individuals. The ideal of self-knowledge as a source of strength and confidence does not imply a selfish or extravagant preoccupation with self. Rather, a time of crisis calls for an examination and appraisal of one's own resources in order to turn one's attention outward again, freshened and fortified by a new inner sureness. As Americans, we can best effect this self-examination, we can best find our true origins, by returning to the words and thoughts of those individuals who have contributed most mightily to our enduring strength. And since most of us lack the special training that would enable us to move unaided with ease in the social and intellectual context of another time, we solicit the help of such people as those who are making the books in this

series—individual author-editors whom we have chosen
for breadth and depth of knowledge and for generosity
of mind and spirit—that they may the better guide us,
through these books, in our self-examination.

HIRAM HAYDN

CONTENTS

CHRONOLOGY

1767—Born in Waxhaw in South Carolina

1780-81—Serves in Revolutionary Army, is captured by the British and is then released

1785-87—Reads law in Salisbury, North Carolina, and is admitted to bar

1788—Settles in Nashville in the Western District of North Carolina

1788—Appointed public prosecutor for the Western District of North Carolina

1791—Marries Rachel Donelson Robards

1791—Appointed attorney general for the Territory South of the River Ohio

1795—Settles at "The Hermitage" as a cotton planter

1796—Serves as delegate to Tennessee constitutional convention

1796—Elected to House of Representatives

1797—Elected to Senate and resigns in following year

1798—Appointed to Superior Court of Tennessee

1802—Elected major-general of Tennessee militia

1804—Resigns from Superior Court of Tennessee

1806—Confers with Aaron Burr on latter's plan for a Western expedition

1806-12—Devotes major attention to his plantation

1812-15—Leads troops against Indians and British in War of 1812

1814—Troops under his command defeat Creeks at Horseshoe Bend

1815—Troops under his command defeat British at New Orleans

1818—Heads Florida expedition

1821—Resigns military commission and becomes first governor of the Florida Territory

1822—Nominated for the Presidency by the Tennessee legislature

1823—Elected to Senate

1824-25—Receives plurality of electoral vote in Presidential election, but loses election to John Quincy Adams in the House of Representatives

1825—Resigns from the Senate

1825-28—His supporters conduct campaign for his election to the Presidency in 1828

1828—Elected President

1829—Introduces spoils system

1830—Vetoes Maysville Road Bill

1830—Obtains British permission for direct United States trade to the British West Indies

1831-36—At his insistence, France agrees to pay United States claims arising from attacks on American commerce

1831—Reorganizes cabinet following Eaton affair and break with John C. Calhoun

1832—Vetoes bill to recharter the Bank of the United States

1832—Issues proclamation on nullification in South Carolina

1833—On his orders Secretary of the Treasury withdraws Federal deposits from the Bank of the United States and places them in state banks

1834—Replies to Senate criticism of his policies with the "Protest"

1836—Issues Specie Circular

1837—Retires to "The Hermitage"

1845—Dies at "The Hermitage"

Part One

JACKSON'S PLACE IN THE AMERICAN TRADITION

JACKSON'S PLACE IN THE
AMERICAN TRADITION

FEW tenets of the American creed have exerted a more pervasive influence on popular thought in the United States than the idea of the free individual. Based on the assumption that man is a rational and evolving creature endowed with the ability to ascertain his own best interests, the concept of individualism depicted man as the master of his own fate and served as the foundation on which Americans erected their theories of progress, *laissez-faire* capitalism and political democracy.

But although Americans have always preached individualism, they have not always practiced it. In the early years of the new republic the interests of many individuals were often subordinated to those of a ruling minority, while in a later period the freedom of every individual was increasingly circumscribed by the demands for conformity imposed by an industrial civilization and a corporate economy.

Andrew Jackson was President of the United States during the golden age of American individualism. An earlier generation of American leaders had talked of equality of opportunity, while reserving to themselves the right to control the nation's government and economy; but by the 1830s it seemed to many people that at last the theory was on the way to becoming a reality. Poor boys—provided that they were able and lucky enough—were becoming rich men; representatives of every class were entering profes-

17

sions that had once been considered the exclusive posses-
sions of the aristocracy; and a local politician and national
military hero from Tennessee had broken the control of
Eastern politicians over the Presidency of the United
States. Jackson and the doctrine of the free individual had
grown up with the new nation, and his rise from humble
birth to the highest office in the land appealed to a people
who believed, not necessarily that all men were equal, but
at least that every man should have an equal right to prove
his superiority.

As President, Jackson not only typified his times; he also
shaped them. By gauging accurately the aspirations of the
American people and translating them into a program that
won their overwhelming support, he increased both his and
their power over the national government. He was the first
President to provide the majority with effective leadership,
and of his successors only Abraham Lincoln, Theodore
Roosevelt, Woodrow Wilson and Franklin Roosevelt were
able to apply those principles that made the "Reign of King
Andrew" synonymous with democracy. Although these
four men had little else in common, they all shared with
Jackson the ability to identify their policies with the interests of the majority and to create the impression that they
and their supporters were masters rather than victims of
the age in which they lived. The merits of Jackson have
been thoroughly debated, but his outstanding contribution
to his and our times was his conclusive demonstration that
"the first principle of our system" of government "is that
the majority is to govern."

Jacksonian Democracy was in some respects an out-
growth of Jeffersonian Republicanism, but the two movements should not be confused. To Jefferson and his fol-

lowers democracy was in part a negative doctrine that often appeared to have no other purpose than to protect the individual against the tyranny of a too-powerful government. Jackson, although never abandoning this idea, shifted its emphasis from the weakness of the state to the strength of the people, so that during his administration democracy became an effective, and at the same time exciting, means by which individuals coalesced behind a forceful and imaginative leader to achieve definite ends. Jefferson thought that a powerful executive might destroy democracy; Jackson demonstrated that a strong President was an essential feature of the American democratic process. Jackson's ability to provide a type of leadership that strengthened rather than vitiated American democracy can be attributed to the skill with which he ascertained and exemplified the will of the majority, his broad view of the national interest, and the extent to which his thought and policies reflected the acquisitive spirit of his times.

I • The Will of the Majority

ALTHOUGH Jackson's name has been repeatedly linked with democracy, he contributed little or nothing to the development of popular rule in the decades that preceded his accession to the Presidency. State after state broadened its suffrage requirements, but Jackson was never even remotely associated with this most fundamental of all democratic practices. The undemocratic Congressional caucus for selecting Presidential candidates gave way to the popularly elected nominating convention; but the Jacksonian Democrats were the last of the three major parties of the period to adopt this new system. Every state but one transferred from the legislature to the voters the right to designate Presidential electors, but there is no evidence that Jackson supported this move to democratize the method for electing the nation's chief executive. Finally, the expansion of educational facilities, the abolition of imprisonment for debt and the adoption of mechanic's lien laws were all products of agitation by middle-class reformers with whom Jackson had no contact before becoming President.

A product of the West, Jackson throughout most of his life gave little indication that he was affected by the democratic influences that many historians have insisted were

21

peculiar to the frontier. As a lawyer, public official, plantation owner, slaveholder, land speculator and merchant,
he belonged to the region's upper class, and he and his
fellow aristocrats formed an oligarchy that frequently controlled their state's political machinery and always domi-
nated its economic life. In national affairs Jackson was a
follower of Jefferson rather than of Washington and Hamilton, but at home in Tennessee he belonged to the small
group of "nabobs" who consistently opposed and repeatedly thwarted the aspirations of the more numerous small
farmers or "leathershirts." While serving as a delegate to
Tennessee's constitutional convention, a Representative in
Congress, a Senator, a member of his state's highest court,
and the first American governor of the Florida territory,
Jackson did not once espouse a policy that was designed
to aid the majority or to weaken the control of the minority
over the government. If, as Frederick Jackson Turner has
asserted, democracy was a product of the frontier, it flour-
ished in that region in spite of the efforts of the nation's
most famous Westerner and the era's most renowned
Democrat.

In his long and illustrious military career Jackson never
showed any marked concern for the rights of the individual or the views of the majority. Whether he was leading
his troops against the British regulars at New Orleans, overwhelming the Indians at Horseshoe Bend or chastising the
Spanish in Florida, he was an extraordinarily harsh disci-
plinarian. He did not hesitate to order the execution of
the rawest recruit for insubordination and—to use one of his
favorite expressions—he would "hang as high as Haman"
those he suspected of dealing with the enemy. It is doubtful if any other American military hero ever possessed

as many attributes of what is commonly called "Prussian-ism" as did Andrew Jackson. And he carried these atti-tudes into civilian life. He repeatedly issued and accepted challenges to duel. When an antagonist seemed unworthy of a contest on the field of honor, Jackson would accost the unfortunate offender in public and cane him. Finally, if all else failed, he did not shrink from an impromptu gun fight such as the battle he waged with the Benton brothers in a Nashville hotel in 1813.

Despite Jackson's apparent lack of concern for either in-dividual or majority rights, he was not altogether immune to the democratic developments that were transforming America. Like most Westerners—and, for that matter, most Americans of his age—he mingled with all classes and was inclined to judge an individual on his merits rather than on his family background and rank in the social hierarchy. He had, moreover, filled a number of government posts which enabled him both to observe and participate in the democratic process. Finally, he was a civilian, not a pro-fessional, soldier. Like Cincinnatus, he took up arms only when his country was threatened, and he invariably re-turned to his plow after the enemy had been repulsed.

Jackson did not become identified with popular govern-ment until relatively late in life, and even then he aligned himself with the democratic movement in much the same fashion as a man who agrees to a marriage of convenience that has been arranged by prudent parents. The circum-stances that made the marriage possible were a series of unexpected developments in the Presidential campaign of 1824; the matchmakers were some of Jackson's influential friends and advisers in Tennessee. Although Jackson in 1816 had stated that he was not "fit to be President," he

changed his mind when the state legislature entered his
name in the campaign of 1824. Because Jackson had not
taken a stand on any of the major issues of the day and
because any stand was bound to alienate some voters, his
campaign managers emphasized his military career, ignored the issues and put him forward as a national hero
who was above the petty disputes of other politicians. Because each of his three opponents—John Quincy Adams,
of Massachusetts, Henry Clay, of Kentucky, and William
H. Crawford, of South Carolina—held an important position in the government and was supported by a powerful
political organization, they were depicted as the favorites
of entrenched minority groups. Jackson, on the other hand,
was described as the candidate of the masses. In this fashion Jackson's backers were able to convince large numbers
of voters—many of whom had only recently been enfran-
chised—that the old soldier from Tennessee was a man of
the people and the ideal representative of the majority in
an age of emergent democracy.

Since Jackson was the only one of the four candidates
to attract any appreciable support outside his own section,
he was able to obtain a plurality in the electoral college.
But the failure of Jackson or any other candidate to poll
a majority of the electoral votes threw the contest to the
House, where Clay was able to use his influence to have
enough of his followers vote for Adams to give the victory
to the New Englander. When Adams then made Clay Secretary of State the Jacksonians accused both of a "corrupt
bargain." From this charge it was only a short step to the
assertion that Jackson, the choice of the people, had been
robbed of the Presidency by the chicanery and undemocratic methods of an unrepresentative minority. This theme

was expounded in countless variations, and within a short time Jackson and democracy had become virtually interchangeable terms. Few politicians have profited more from defeat than did Jackson in 1824. Entering the campaign as a military hero, he had emerged from the struggle as a symbol of democracy.

Throughout Adams' administration Jackson's supporters sought to insure a victory in the election of 1828 by refighting the campaign of 1824. The "corrupt bargain" was rehashed in editorials, pamphlets and speeches in an effort to demonstrate that Adams, a minority candidate, had stolen the Presidency from the choice of the majority. At the same time, Jackson's campaign managers avoided any discussion of the economic issues that had divided the country's major sections. In the West Jackson was described as a frontiersman; in the South it was emphasized that he was a plantation owner and slaveholder; and in the Northeast he was depicted as a friend of the common man. The success of these tactics was revealed by Jackson's sweeping victory over Adams in 1828. Many Westerners voted for Jackson because they looked on him as one of their own; Southerners, however much they were disturbed by his appeals to the masses, preferred him to Adams, who advocated a type of nationalism that seemed a threat to their section's most vital interests; and in the Northeast he had the support of machines—such as Martin Van Buren's Albany Regency—and of numerous voters who for whatever reasons opposed the groups in power.

If political expediency was the principal reason for Jackson's conversion to the democratic faith, this fact had no effect on the enthusiasm with which he preached and practiced the new creed during his two terms as President.

Throughout his administration he viewed himself as the agent of the majority and as a chief executive who derived as much power from the people as from the Constitution. Other Presidents had been content to administer the laws enacted by Congress, but Jackson not only helped to make the laws, he also convinced the majority that he was making them with its assistance and for its benefit. The result was that countless individuals who had previously thought of themselves as being ruled by the government for the first time believed that they were ruling themselves. But Jackson gave the voters who supported him more than a sense of participation, for he also provided them with the leadership that could make the majority an effective factor in national politics.

Jackson's success as a Presidential leader can be attributed in large part to his ability to ascertain the will of the majority and to translate this knowledge into a policy that all could understand regardless of conflicting opinions on its merits. Whether he was battling Nicholas Biddle and Henry Clay over the Bank of the United States, insisting to his cabinet members and to the nation that the wife of the Secretary of War was "as chaste as a virgin," vetoing an internal-improvement bill that was favored by his Western constituents, or threatening to hang the leaders of the South Carolina nullification movement, he could count on overwhelmingly popular support. His genius as a spokesman for the majority lay not only in his ability to rally the people to his support, but also in the skill with which he perceived how the masses would react to any particular question before that question had been raised. He did not so much direct or form public opinion as stay one step ahead of it. Thus, he was a leader who, while giving the

impression of commanding his followers, actually led them
in the direction that they, without quite realizing it, had
always wanted to go. It was this ability both to reflect and
affect public opinion that made Jackson the first President
to rule by popular support. Moreover, his successors in the
White House who have not shared this ability with him
have gone down in history—and rightfully so—as medioc-
rities.

In taking a stand on any issue Jackson did not attempt
first to find out which way the prevailing winds of public
opinion were blowing and then set his course accordingly.
Unlike some modern politicians who cannot advocate or
reject a policy until they have studied the latest Gallup
Poll, he always assumed that a majority of the voters would
agree with him. And events usually proved him right. Jackson was not a designing politician—he did not have to
be. He could afford to follow his instincts, for they seldom
failed him.

Once having settled on a course of action, Jackson reduced the question to its essentials, explained his position
in forthright terms and accused his opponents of plotting
to destroy individual freedom and to block the will of
the majority. His political adversaries, who at first were
astounded by this strategy, became enraged and bitter
when they finally realized how conclusively they had been
defeated. Politicians like Clay, Calhoun and Webster, unable either to check or comprehend the forces that over-
whelmed them, blamed their repeated setbacks on the
unreasoning adulation of the unthinking masses for a dem-
agogic, headstrong autocrat. What they failed to understand—and what their twentieth-century counterparts have
not yet learned—is that a powerful President derives his

power not by fooling the people, but by making a sustained effort to satisfy their needs and aspirations.

The spoils system provided the minority with the first evidence of the nature of Jacksonian Democracy. Although Jackson dismissed far fewer government employees than most of his contemporaries imagined and although he did not originate the spoils system, he made more sweeping changes in the Federal bureaucracy than had any of his predecessors. What is even more significant is that he defended these changes as a positive good. At present when the use of political patronage is generally considered an obstacle to good government, it is worth remembering that Jackson and his followers invariably described rotation in public office as a "reform." In this sense the spoils system was more than a way to reward Jackson's friends and punish his enemies; it was also a device for removing from public office the representatives of minority political groups that Jackson insisted had been made corrupt by their long tenure. In its initial stages Jacksonian Democracy had developed as a movement to place the choice of the majority in the nation's highest elective office. On assuming power the Jacksonians insisted that appointive as well as elective offices belonged to members of that party whose numerical strength had given them control over the executive branch of the government. If nothing else, the spoils system demonstrated that positions in the Federal government were no longer the private preserve of a small and unrepresentative group of insiders.

The spoils system filled the executive branch of the government with representatives of the majority—who, of course, were also members of Jackson's party—but it did not give the majority an opportunity to participate in national affairs at the policy-making level. In the war on the bank, however, Jackson demonstrated that the people could be an important and even decisive factor in the legislative process. When Congress in 1832 adopted a bill rechartering the Second Bank of the United States, Jackson vetoed the measure. In his veto message he described the issue as a contest between the few and the many, and took his stand unequivocally on the side of the many. To Jackson it was a question of whether the nation's banking and financial affairs should be controlled by a small but powerful minority group with confederates in Congress or by the people with the President as their spokesman. Friends of the bank maintained that its constitutionality had been established by the Supreme Court, but Jackson replied that this was little better than an irrelevancy. The Justices could speak for themselves but they could not speak for the President. Nor was the President compelled to carry out the wishes of Congress when they conflicted with the interests of the people. Jackson, in effect, maintained that the executive was not only an autonomous part of the government but that it was also the most important part, and it occupied this position because it alone was responsive to the wishes of a majority of the voters. Implicit, if not explicit, in Jackson's statement was his conviction that the Justices of the Supreme Court spoke only for themselves, that the members of Congress reflected the interests of factions and that he alone represented the people.

Congress sustained Jackson's veto, and the voters gave their overwhelming approval to his program in the Presidential election of 1832. Convinced anew of both the righteousness and the popularity of his course, Jackson decided that the time had come to destroy the bank by having the Secretary of the Treasury transfer the government's deposits to the state, or "pet," banks. When the Senate censured him for this move he replied with the "Protest," in which he defended the constitutionality of the removal of the deposits, castigated the Senate for attempting to interfere with the conduct of the executive branch of the government, reiterated his theory of Presidential leadership, declared that he was "the direct representative of the American People," and "solemnly" protested against the "proceedings of the Senate as unauthorized by the Constitution, contrary to its spirit and to several of its express provisions, subversive of that distribution of the powers of government which it has ordained and established, destructive of the checks and safeguards by which those powers were intended on the one hand to be controlled and on the other to be protected, and calculated by their immediate and collateral effects, by their character and tendency, to concentrate in the hands of a body not directly amenable to the people a degree of influence and power dangerous to their liberties and fatal to the Constitution of their choice."

Jackson's war on the bank provides an outstanding, but nevertheless typical, example of the techniques he employed as a Presidential leader. Throughout the controversy he repeatedly defeated a hostile Congress by taking his case to the people. When a majority of the voters responded to his leadership by supporting his program, he was in a position to exert an influence that was far greater than that exercised by any of his predecessors in the White House. He had, in short, discovered the source of Presidential power, and in so doing he had made the executive the most important branch of the government and the majority the most significant factor in the nation's politics.

II • The National Interest

HISTORIANS have consumed large amounts of paper and printers' ink in a debate over the extent to which Jackson's policies reflected the interests of the nation's various sections. For many years students of American history agreed that both Jackson and his policies were products of the frontier. But this view has recently been challenged by those who insist that he steadfastly adhered to a program which aided the poorer classes of the Northeast. Scholars in both camps have been belligerent enough to have gained the approval of Jackson himself, but they have also assigned to him roles that he repeatedly refused to play. To his mind he was neither a Westerner nor Easterner, but an American; and in an age in which every other major political figure represented a sectional interest, Jackson consistently sought to represent the national interest.

Those who believe that Jacksonian Democracy was distinctly Western in both its origins and manifestations emphasize Jackson's early life, his personal attributes and the consistency with which he was supported by voters in states beyond the Alleghenies. After pointing out that he had always lived on or close to the frontier, they conclude that his experiences in the West played a major part in shaping his attitude toward the issues that confronted his administration. This point is given added plausibility by frequent references to his allegedly Western traits, and readers are constantly reminded that he was hot-tempered, individualistic and bellicose. Although this interpretation makes Jackson a product of the West, it does not do the same for his administration, for it overlooks the fact that in many instances he was popular in his own section in spite of, not because of, his policies.

Historians who contend that Jackson was a Westerner with Eastern attitudes devote their major attention to his economic policies and to the writings of many contemporary Eastern radicals. According to this interpretation, the war on the bank was supported by the poorer members of American society in both the East and the West, but the administration's hard-money program antagonized Westerners and was endorsed by Eastern workingmen. To substantiate this view quotations from pamphlets by Eastern reformers are cited as proof of Jackson's popularity among the nation's laboring classes. At the same time much is made of the fact that Martin Van Buren, of New York, became the administration's crown prince. These points, however, are far from conclusive, for they fail to emphasize that Jackson's advocacy of hard money was only one of his many policies; that Eastern radicals did not necessarily speak for either the workingman or for Jackson; and that if Van Buren was a close political associate of the President, so was—to mention only one example—Thomas Hart Benton, of Missouri.

The fact that historians have been unable to agree on the exact nature of Jackson's sectional affiliations is in itself an indication of his national-mindedness. While any measure that he sponsored inevitably aided some parts of the country more than it did others, he never saw his program in this light. The war on the bank, for example, was a product of his economic thought rather than a bid for votes in the North, South or West. In similar fashion his veto of the Maysville Road Bill (which provided Federal assistance for the construction of a road in Kentucky) was based on a constitutional interpretation that ignored the sectional implications of the issue. By insisting that the Maysville Road was a local rather than a national undertaking, he presumably antagonized some of his Western supporters, but on numerous other occasions he won their approval by backing internal improvements that cut across state lines. Finally, when he opposed South Carolina's nullification of the tariff, he aligned himself with the very Northern groups that had consistently attacked his stand on the hard-money and bank questions. Each of Jackson's policies may be interpreted from a sectional viewpoint, but a different interpretation is needed for each policy, for he stubbornly refused to allow one section either to dominate or to defy his administration. He viewed the United States not as a collection of sections, but as a community of free individuals who were bound together by common interests and a common nationality.

When Jackson became President in 1829, his cabinet contained representatives from each of the major sections, and the administration seemed to stand for nothing but his conviction that he deserved to be President. The new regime, which many had thought would produce revolutionary changes, gave every indication that it would follow a well-established pattern of government by compromise in which attempts would be made to hold the allegiance of the North, South and West by a series of ingenious intersectional swaps or trades. But this period of relative calm ended abruptly when Jackson decided to defend the

morals of a tavernkeeper's daughter who also happened
to be the wife of Secretary of War John W. Eaton. When
the wives of the other cabinet members (only Van Buren,
who was a widower, was wifeless) refused to treat Peggy
Eaton as a social equal, Jackson made her cause an administration policy, threatened and cajoled his wife-ridden department heads, and as a last resort dismissed all of them.
Throughout the controversy some of his more courageous
advisers dared to tell him that Peggy's reputation was not
altogether undeserved and warned him that the "Eaton
trouble" was so ludicrous and degrading that it was be-
neath the notice of the President of the United States.

They were right, of course, but of far greater historical
significance is the fashion in which Jackson demonstrated
that he was willing to destroy a coalition—no matter how
essential it seemed to his political career—whose members
did not reflect his wishes. The sectional and political implications of Jackson's stand were of far-reaching importance, for the most prominent member of the coalition was
Vice President John C. Calhoun, the undisputed spokesman of the Old South and the husband of the woman who
had led the cabinet wives in their campaigns against Peggy.
Jackson, in effect, had risked alienating the representative
of one of the nation's major sections because a woman had
not been treated as a lady. The issue that he thus established as a test of administration loyalty was altogether
trivial, but it was this fact that made Jackson's opposition
to Calhoun even more significant than it otherwise would
have been.

Jackson achieved his most impressive victory over par-
ticularism in his struggle with South Carolina on the nullification of the tariff of 1832. Although the nullification

crisis marked the culmination of a bitter personal feud between Jackson and Calhoun, this fact should not obscure the fundamental issues that were involved. Stripped of verbiage—it was Calhoun who supplied most of the verbiage and Jackson who did all the stripping—the question was whether a state could refuse to obey a Federal statute or, in a larger sense, whether a part of the Union was more powerful than the Union itself. Calhoun, going beyond the theory of States' rights, asserted that because the states had made the Constitution they could pass on the constitutionality of an act of Congress, and that if the original compact which the states had drawn up was violated, they were no longer bound by the agreement and could withdraw from the Union. But Jackson, refusing to accept either Calhoun's premise or conclusions, maintained that the Constitution had been created not by the states but by individuals, that the United States was not a federation of autonomous units, and that the Union was indestructible. Between these two positions there was no middle ground.

To Jackson, Calhoun's theories were nonsense; they were, moreover, a kind of nonsense that he was prepared to suppress with force as soon as anyone sought to apply them. When in July 1832 South Carolina's delegation to Congress adopted a resolution urging the nullification of the tariff, Jackson said: "They can talk and write resolutions and print threats to their hearts' content. But if one drop of blood be shed there in defiance of the laws of the United States I will hang the first man of them I can get my hands on to the first tree I can find."

But the leaders of the rebellious state refused to heed this warning, and in November 1832 South Carolina adopted an

ordinance which nullified the tariffs of 1828 and 1832 and
warned that any attempt to collect the duties under either
act would lead to the state's secession from the Union. Jackson, who had meanwhile strengthened the Federal government's military establishment in South Carolina, replied to
the ordinance of nullification with a proclamation that was
written by Secretary of State Edward Livingston but expressed the President's convictions on the inviolability of
the Union. After reviewing the history of the Articles of
Confederation and the Constitution, the proclamation declared "the power to annul a law of the United States, assumed by one State, incompatible with the existence of the
Union, contradicted expressly by the letter of the Constitution, unauthorized by its spirit, inconsistent with every
principle on which it was founded, and destructive of the
great object for which it was formed." The Constitution
created "a government, not a league." It was, moreover, "a
Government in which all the people are represented, which
operates directly on the people individually, not upon the
States." As a consequence, secession was a "revolutionary
act" rather than a "constitutional right." Although Jackson
begged the citizens of South Carolina to repudiate the nullificationists, he also made it clear that he would go to any
extreme to uphold the Union. He had "no discretionary
power on the subject," for "disunion by armed force" was
"*treason,*" and as "First Magistrate" of the United States
he would not "avoid the performance of his duty."

Throughout the controversy between the Federal government and South Carolina, Jackson was not only a nationalist but also the Presidential leader of the majority.
While Calhoun used the allegedly unique interests of his
state and section to demand what in effect was minority

rule, Jackson based the government's authority on forces that transcended both state and sectional lines. In this respect Jackson's role was essentially the same as that in the war against the bank when he spoke for a majority—regardless of where its members lived—against a minority that happened to be centered in the Northeast. This concept of the Presidency left no room for the idea that the United States was a product of a compact drawn up by autonomous states; for, if each state was sovereign, the majority would be fractionalized until it had become impotent. In combating Calhoun's theories, Jackson was defending not only the Union but also his own concept of the President's duties and functions as the representative of the people.

Because the nullification struggle was ended by a Compromise Tariff and a Force Act that was nullified by South Carolina, the President's opponents claimed the victory. Jackson himself readily admitted that he had checked rather than crushed the nullification movement, and in April 1833 he wrote to a friend: "The nullifiers in the south intend to blow up a storm on the slave question. . . . This ought to be met, for be assured these men would do any act to destroy this union and form a southern confederacy bounded, north, by the Potomac river." But Jackson had nevertheless achieved his major objective. He had successfully upheld the Union, and the nullificationists in all likelihood owed their lives to the fact that they had for whatever reasons failed to carry out their plans. Nor can the outcome of the dispute obscure the stand that had been consistently maintained by Jackson. He stood for nationalism against localism, majority rule against minority rule, and the concept of a government created and maintained by individuals against Calhoun's theory of a league of vir-

tually sovereign states. He had, in short, preserved both
the Union and the rights of the individuals who comprised
it. In Jackson's mind the two were indistinguishable.

In seeking to safeguard the Union, Jackson did not attempt to crush the states. As a follower of Thomas Jefferson he had supported the States' rights doctrines of the
Kentucky and Virginia Resolutions of 1798, and for the remainder of his life he opposed the Federalist views on the
desirability of a highly centralized government. In his mes-
sages to Congress he repeatedly warned against attempts
to increase the power of the national government at the
expense of the states and insisted that Federal authority
should never transcend the limits imposed on it by the Constitution. In addition, many of his policies either directly
or indirectly enhanced state prestige and authority. Thus,
he vetoed a bill calling for a subsidy for an internal improvement within a state, transferred the Federal deposits
from a central bank to institutions under state jurisdiction,
and inaugurated a plan for the distribution among the various states of the surplus in the Federal Treasury. But in
upholding the rights of the states, he had no intention of
undermining the rights of the central government, and it
was on this point that he clashed with the nullificationists.
Calhoun believed that a state government was a product
of the people, but that the Federal government was a product of the states; Jackson maintained that "both [state and
Federal] Governments are the Governments of the people." Calhoun, by advocating state sovereignty, had to end
up by preaching disunion. Jackson, by defending States'
rights, could logically uphold both the states and the Union.

In foreign as in domestic affairs Jackson was an invet-
erate and outspoken champion of the sovereignty of the

United States and the rights of the American people. A patriot, he lived as well as preached his creed. He served in the Revolution as a thirteen-year-old boy, commanded the troops that defeated the British at New Orleans and led a punitive expedition against the Spanish in Florida. As President he was an equally staunch defender of his country's honor, and at his insistence France paid claims that dated back to 1803 and Great Britain opened its West Indian trade to American vessels for the first time since the Revolution. Although the agreements reached with Great Britain and France were relatively minor diplomatic triumphs, they ended two disputes of long standing and furnished evidence of Jackson's determination to uphold the prestige of the United States government in Europe as well as at home.

Unlike many modern nationalists, Jackson was neither a nativist nor a reactionary. His nationalism was an inextricable part of his concept of majority rule by free individuals, and it required neither loyalty oaths nor investigating committees to test the Americanism of his fellow Americans. He believed that the Union was indissoluble and that the interests of the majority provided the only true index to the national interest. In Jackson's day these ideas were bitterly opposed by influential and respected Americans; today they are basic tenets of the American democratic creed.

III • The Acquisitive Spirit

WHEN Jackson became President, the United States had just entered a period of rapid and unprecedented economic development. New England's factory towns were beginning to rival its ports as centers of employment and investment, while the Middle Atlantic states had a diversified economy in which the region's shipping, financial, manufacturing and agricultural interests played more or less complementary roles. Although the Upper South had fallen on hard times and tobacco culture had exhausted much of its soil, the Black Belt in the Deep South had already become the world's major source of cotton and the home of the antebellum plantation system. In the West an expanding economy provided opportunities for grain growers, corn and hog farmers, land speculators and sponsors of a wide variety of internal improvements. In sum, the United States had entered the age of enterprise from which it has not yet emerged.

European visitors to the United States during the Age of Jackson almost without exception commented on the extraordinary materialism of the American people. Americans seemed to exist for no other reason than to make money or to talk about making it. Nor were Americans ashamed of this, for what foreigners condemned as materialism Americans praised as enterprise. Moreover, Americans suspected—no doubt with some justification—that Old

World critics secretly envied what they professed to despise. Thus, it was not that Americans were more materialistic than other peoples, but that they had an unexampled opportunity to devote themselves to materialist goals. Americans were not different but the United States was, for apparently limitless resources, the absence of an hereditary aristocracy and the inability of any single economic group to control the government for its own interests gave everyone a chance to make a fortune. America, like Europe, had its class divisions, but it did not have Europe's class rigidity.

The United States possessed not only an expanding economy, but also a ready-made economic philosophy that seemed to Americans both to explain and sanction the fashion in which their economy functioned. When Adam Smith published the *Wealth of Nations* in 1776, he was writing a tract that was designed to win people over to his version of the ideal organization for a national economy; but to Americans in the 1830s his words described what was, rather than what should be. If Americans did not always practice the economic theories they preached, they always believed what they preached. Few doubted that the individual was the best judge of his own interests and that if left to pursue them he would promote both his own and the general welfare. Few, moreover, doubted the wisdom of letting the individual pursue his interests without governmental interference. And finally, few doubted that in economics, as in politics, the victors got and deserved the spoils, while the losers got what they deserved.

Jackson both understood and approved the American economic system, for he was one of its more distinguished products. Starting life as a poor boy, he ended it as a large

plantation owner and member of the upper class. His
life, like that of so many others in his generation, demonstrated that the American dream could also be a reality.
Although he was often in need of ready cash and never
free from financial worries, the wealth he had accumu-
lated could be measured in other ways than by money.
He owned more than a hundred slaves, kept a stable of
racing horses (which he transferred to Washington when
he became President), was justifiably proud of his wine
cellar, supported a veritable army of indigent in-laws and
had one of the most imposing homes in Tennessee. In ris-
ing from log cabin to White House, he had repeatedly
displayed those qualities of industry and initiative that
everyone agreed were essential to individual success. In
his relentless search for the main chance he had been merchant, lawyer, planter, speculator and officeholder. He
could, and did, drive a hard bargain, and he believed in
the Calvinistic doctrine of the efficacy of hard work. In
every respect he was a representative figure of the acquisitive age in which he lived.

As a well-to-do member of Tennessee's ruling class, Jackson repeatedly opposed the efforts of the poorer classes to
enlist the aid of the state government. In 1817 he and his
fellow creditors successfully checked the debtors' demands
for the adoption of a stay law (or moratorium), supported
the hard-money policy of the Bank of the United States,
attacked the $50,000 annual tax that the state imposed on
the bank's branches, and condemned the indiscriminate
fashion in which Tennessee chartered independent banks
that flooded the region with paper money. In later years
Jackson was to change his attitude toward the Bank of the
United States, but he never abandoned his hard-money

views and he never altered his conviction that it was not the function of a government to assist any economic group.

Jackson was a man of his time, and his economic views cannot be made to fit a twentieth-century society for which they were not designed. Unlike most modern liberals he did not believe that the government should regulate the nation's economic affairs, and unlike most modern conservatives he did not advocate a type of *laissez faire* that permitted corporate enterprise to ignore virtually all the tenets of *laissez faire*. A product of an economy that consisted of many small units rather than a few large ones, he thought that the government could intervene to prevent a vested interest from using its power to thwart what were considered the legitimate aspirations of less powerful but more numerous members of the nation's economy. But, having done this, the government was under no obligation to assist those who lacked the ability to take advantage of the opportunities that nature—with the government's connivance—had made available to all. Every man was considered the architect of his own destiny, and if he bungled the job he had no one to blame but himself. Jackson had not bungled the job, and he never thought that the government should aid those who had.

Jackson's theories on the role of the government in the economy have little or nothing in common with the ideas propounded by modern advocates of the positive state; and those historians who have attempted to demonstrate that the Age of Jackson was the precursor of the New Deal have been forced to ignore the meaning of both his words and his times. A Jeffersonian by background and inclination, he feared big government as much as, if not more than, he feared big business. He did not believe the government could do whatever was not expressly forbidden by the Constitution, and he repeatedly warned individuals and states that their rights would be jeopardized by any unconstitutional extension of Federal authority. Throughout his administration he maintained that "the successful operation of the federal system" could "only be preserved by confining it to the few and simple, but yet important, objects for which it was designed," and that such objects were "limited to a general superintending power to maintain peace at home and abroad, and to prescribe laws on a few subjects of general interest not calculated to restrict human liberty, but to enforce human rights."

On assuming the Presidency Jackson did not consider himself the spokesman of any class. In his thinking, as in that of most of his contemporaries, class distinctions marked gradations of wealth but not differences in individual interests. Because all people, regardless of wealth, presumably shared the motives of Adam Smith's economic man, they viewed their problems from an individual standpoint rather than from that of the class to which they belonged. Jackson did not object to some people being rich and others being poor, for in a competitive society this was both inevitable and desirable. He did, however, object to man-made restrictions on individual initiative and man-made limitations on economic competition, for these prevented everyone from having an equal opportunity to get rich. A typical nineteenth-century liberal, he voiced the aspirations of the nation's artisans, small farmers and small businessmen, all of whom hoped that they too could someday be wealthy. These groups may or may not have belonged to the middle class, but there can be no doubt that they all had middle-class ideals. They asked only for what all considered an inalienable right—the right to get ahead.

The Second Bank of the United States was an obvious target for a man of Jackson's economic views. Although he had supported the bank in 1817, he had done so largely because of its hard-money program, and in subsequent years he came increasingly to believe that its unchecked power had made it the strongest and most dangerous monopoly in the land. Whether the bank was a monopoly is perhaps debatable, but it undeniably was a privileged institution and it had obtained its privileges from the government. Because of its control over both currency and credit, it was in a position to make or break other banks, to retard or stimulate economic activity in the various sections of the country, and to play an influential part in determining the ups and downs of the business cycle. Five of its twenty-five directors were appointed by the government, but in effect neither the government nor the people could control its policies. The bank conflicted with both Jackson's economic and political theories, and it was for this reason that he decided, first, to block its efforts to obtain a new charter and, then, to destroy it before its present charter had expired.

In his first annual message to Congress, Jackson questioned "both the constitutionality and the expediency of the law creating this bank." A year later he referred to "the dangers which many of our citizens apprehend from that institution as at present organized" and to the bank's ability "to operate on the hopes, fears, or interests of large masses of the community." In his veto message he attacked the bank from every quarter, charging that it was a monopoly, that it was owned in part by foreign interests, that it was

unconstitutional, that it had violated the terms of its charter, that its profits accrued to those who controlled it rather
than to the people, that it exercised its power arbitrarily,
and that it was both a menace and an anomaly in a democratic society. It was not, however, until his concluding
paragraphs that he stated his view of the government's role
in the economy. Conceding that "distinctions in society
will always exist under every just government," he condemned "laws undertake[n] to add to these natural and
just advantages artificial distinctions, to grant titles, gratuities, and exclusive privileges, to make the rich richer and
the potent more powerful." If the government "would
confine itself to equal protection, and as Heaven does its
rains, shower its favors alike on the high and the low, the
rich and the poor, it would be an unqualified blessing." But
the government had ignored this principle when it granted
a new charter to the bank, and by attempting to make
"many of our rich men . . . richer by act of Congress" it
had "arrayed section against section, interest against interest, and man against man, in a fearful commotion which
threatens to shake the foundations of our Union."

Following the withdrawal of the government's funds,
both the Bank of the United States and the independent
banks issued large amounts of notes that were not backed
by specie. Jackson was convinced that the speculative
boom that developed after 1834 was caused by these unrestricted note issues, and he repeatedly demanded that
the nation's currency be based on gold and silver. Responding to Jackson's requests, Congress adopted measures
to increase the supply of coins in the circulating medium.
But these steps were taken too late to check the boom, and
the states refused to make any move to curb the inflationist

policies of the banks in their jurisdiction. Jackson, however, was not altogether powerless in this situation, and in 1836 he issued the Specie Circular, ordering that all payments for government lands be made in specie or in notes of specie-paying banks.

Jackson viewed his hard-money policies as a continuation of the program he had inaugurated with his attacks on the bank, for he believed the issue of bank notes was still another method by which a privileged minority was using its power to deprive the majority of its legitimate economic rights. While financiers were in a position to profit in the period of speculative prosperity they had created, the rest of the population saw its real income decline as prices increased. In his annual message of 1834 Jackson stated that "our gold coinage" would make the United States "as little liable to fluctuations as any other commercial country." In the following year he stated "the great desideratum in modern times is an efficient check upon the power of banks, preventing that excessive issue of paper whence arise those fluctuations in the standard of value which render uncertain the rewards of labor"; and in 1836 he warned that the uncontrolled issue of bank notes meant that "prices must vary according to the tide of bank issues, and the value and stability of property must stand exposed to all the uncertainty which attends the administration of institutions that are constantly liable to the temptation of an interest distinct from that of the community in which they are established." Finally, in his "Farewell Address" he said:

The mischief springs from the power which the moneyed interest derives from a paper currency which they are able to control, from the multitude of corporations with exclusive privileges which they have succeeded in obtaining in the different States, and which are employed altogether for their benefit; and unless you become more watchful in your States and check this spirit of monopoly and thirst for exclusive privileges you will in the end find that the most important powers of Government have been given or bartered away, and the control over your dearest interests has passed into the hands of these corporations.

It is impossible to demonstrate that Jackson's hard-money or economic policies reflected the interests of the nation's laboring classes or that his program was viewed in this light by such groups. A working class, as we understand the term today, did not exist in Jackson's day, for both the factory system and the union movement were in their infancy. Moreover, recent research has conclusively shown that almost all the so-called workingmen's leaders who supported Jackson's program were middle or upper-class reformers without any organized following among the low-income groups. In addition, a series of studies on election returns in the country's major cities has revealed that the working-class wards usually voted against the Jacksonian Democrats. Nor is there evidence to support the contention that Jackson had any particular interest for the workers as a class. Although he frequently referred to the welfare of the workingman in his public statements, he always did so in terms that were broad enough to include virtually everyone who worked for a living. The record reveals that on the only occasion when he took sides in a labor dispute, he used the power of the government to crush a strike. There is no reason to believe that Jackson looked with any more favor on organized labor than he did on organized capital.

Jackson was a product of a new nation situated on the edge of a wilderness. His America was not ours, and his policies were fashioned to meet the needs of his, not our, generation. His views on economic individualism, which many of his contemporaries considered radical, have become the last refuge of the modern conservative, and his theories on the nature of the Union seem almost irrelevant to a nation that has not been threatened by disunion for almost a century. Despite these facts, his contribution to American democracy remains. Democracy's battles are never won, its wars never finished, and Jackson's conception of majority rule is as vital and meaningful today as it was in the golden age of American individualism.

Part Two

DOCUMENTS: JACKSON AND HIS TIMES

DOCUMENTS: JACKSON
AND HIS TIMES

ANDREW JACKSON was neither a polished writer nor a profound thinker. His letters contain errors in grammar and spelling; he had to rely on his advisers either to write or rewrite many of his official statements; and the ideas he advanced were far from original. Despite these facts, Jackson's public and private papers comprise a record that cannot be ignored by anyone wishing to understand the nation's early military history, the rise of political democracy in the United States, the growth of Presidential power, the role of the states and the sections in the Federal Union, and the development of American capitalism during its formative stages.

Jackson's writings reveal that he consistently reflected the main currents of American thought and that he knew how to present his ideas so that everyone could understand them. He wrote the way he lived—his prose is straightforward and vigorous. He used adjectives and adverbs sparingly, and he often achieved that "plain easy stile" and "chasteness" of expression that he so admired in Madison. He was never distracted by irrelevancies, and his ability to strip a question down to its essentials made him a far more effective writer than most of his more learned contemporaries in public life.

The documents in this volume are designed to explain and illuminate both Jackson and his times. The selections have been arranged in topical groupings, but within each

53

section the selections have been placed in chronological order. In accord with the usual practice the punctuation and spelling of the public documents have been modernized. On the other hand, the letters have been reproduced virtually as they were written.

I ⋆ The Righteousness of the Sword

I. "THE DISASTER OF OUR ARMY"

JACKSON began his military career when he was a boy and did not end it until he was in his fifties. In 1780, when he was thirteen years old, he joined the Patriot forces in the American Revolution as a "mounted orderly or messenger." In the following year he was captured by the British and imprisoned at Camden, South Carolina, where he witnessed a battle in which a Revolutionary army was defeated. His memorandum on the battle was written in 1843.

Jackson's Memorandum on His Imprisonment at Camden, S. C.*

IN THE MONTH of april 1781 I was a prisoner with the British, confined in Camden Jail, which was then included in the British Redoubt nearest Hobkirks Hill, & Loggtown when Genl Green with his army advanced upon Camden, & encamped upon Hobkirks hill. I with others, were confined in the second story of the Jail, & in the room, overlooking Genl Greens encampment out of its north windows.

---

* From the microfilm collection of the Jackson MSS. in Butler Library, Columbia University. The original of this memorandum is in the Jackson MSS. in the Library of Congress.

A few days after Genl Greens approach an american soldier in the evening was seen coming in from the american
lines, to the redoubt where we were confined, supposed to
be a deserter—soon after his arrival, there appeared considerable stir amongst the British troops, & we began to
fear that a retreat during the ensuing night was intended—
about sunset a carpenter with some soldiers came into our
room with plank, & nailed up the windows looking toward
Genl Greens encampment; some tories who were in company, abused us very much, told us Green was on their
lines without artillery, & they intended to make a second
Gates of him, & hang us all. When night closed, we heard
much bustle in the Garrison, & soon found that the effectives were removing, & the invalids relieving them, from
which we inferred their intention to attack Genl Green in
the morning or attempt to surprise him before day—being
anxious to see the Battle, if one took place, having only a
razor blade which was allowed us to divide our rations
with, I fell to work to cut out a pine Knot, out of the plank
nailed over the windows, obstructing the view of Greens
encampment, and with aid of a fellow prisoner, compleated
my object before day, making an aperture about an inch &
half in diameter which gave a full view of Genl Greens
situation—so soon in the morning as objects could be distinguished, the British army was seen drawn up in column,
under cover of the stockade & Col Kershaws houses—a little after sunrise were seen to move a South east direction,
keeping themselves under cover from a view from Greens
encampment; it continued this direction, untill it reached
the woods, when it wheeled to the left, under cover of the
woods, untill it reached the cheraw road, here it recd. a
severe fire from the american piquet, & was seen to halt for

a moment, when it was again seen to advance and the american piquet retiring keeping up a brisk fire of musquetry—soon after this, the British were seen advancing in order of Battle up the Hill, & Genl Green forming on the hights. The British supposing Green had no artillery, the officers in front lead on their men encourageing them, when Greens battery opened upon them with great effect, many horses coming in with out riders, & many with the wounded upon them & the noncombatants running, helter, skelter, for safety—soon the small arms were heard, & a general action appeared to commence, when the american squadron of horse were seen to charge them on their left & rear, & cut off the retreat of the British from their redoubts—never were hearts elated more than ours, at the glitter of the americans swords, wielded by the american arm so successfully which promised immediate release to us, having cut off the left of the British army which as appeared, he had perfectly in his power if Green had been able to have sustained himself in his position—how short was our Joy, for soon thereafter the roar of the cannon ceased, the sound of our small arms appeared retiring, & the cavalry appeared to be attacked in front *vigorously*, & his only alternative to cut his way thro the enemy, which appeared to be done with great gallantry and retired out of view. The firing having ceased, Capt Smith of the artillery was brought in a prisoner and lodged in the room with us, who related to us the disaster of our army—he had reached Genl Green Just before day, had thrown himself down to rest, in his shirt & drawers, in which he was taken not having time, after the alarm given, to put on his cloaths; Capt Smith said his command was entirely killed or taken but he saved the pieces.

A few days after this battle, I, with six others were exchanged, I traversed the battle ground, found many musquets without their locks, with their bayonets stuck in the earth with their butts up, & some barrells out of their stocks. every appearence indicated a sudden unexpected attack and when many were cleaning their arms etc., etc. Thus unprepared, & one Regiment giving way when ordered to charge the enemy, compelled the other to retreat which left washington in the perilous situation described & compelled him to seek safety by cutting his way through the lines of his enemy which he appear'd to do gallantly.

II. "The Season for Martial Exploits"

After being elected a major general of the Tennessee militia, Jackson waited impatiently for an opportunity to lead his troops into battle. As relations between Great Britain and the United States deteriorated, Jackson's spirits rose proportionately; and when Congress in February 1812 authorized the enlistment of 50,000 volunteers, he welcomed the chance to appeal to his division for volunteers.

Division Orders*

VOLUNTEERS TO ARMS

Citizens! Your goverment has at last yielded to the impulse of the nation. Your impatience is no longer restrained. The hour of national vengeance is now at hand. The eternal enemies of american prosperity are again to

---

* From the microfilm collection of the Jackson MSS. in Butler Library, Columbia University. The original of these orders is in the Jackson MSS. in the Library of Congress.

be taught to respect your rights, after having been compelled to feel, once more, the power of your arms.

War is on the point of breaking out between the united States and the King of great Britain! and the martial hosts of america are summoned to the Tented Fields!

Citizens! An honourable confidence in your courage and your patriotism has been displayed by the general goverment. To raise a force for the protection of your rights she has not deemed it necessary to recur to the common mode of filling the ranks of an army. No drafts or compulsory levies are now to be made.

A simple invitation is given to the young men of the country to arm for their own and their countries rights. On this invitation 50,000 volunteers, full of martial ardor, indignant at their countries wrongs and burning with impatience to illustrate their names by some signal exploit, are expected to repair to the national standard.

Could it be otherwise? Could the general goverment deem it necessary to force *us* to take the field? We, who for so many years have demanded a war with such clamorous importunity—who, in so many resolutions of town meetings and legislative assemblies, have offerred our lives and fortunes for the defence of our country—who, so often and so publickly, have charged this verry goverment with a pusillanimous deference to foreign nations, because she had resolved to exhaust the arts of negociation before she made her last appeal to the power of arms. No under such circumstances it was impossible for the goverment to conceive that compulsion would be wanting to bring us into the field. And shall we now disappoint the expectations which we ourselves have excited? Shall we give the lie to the professions which we have so often and so publickly

made? Shall we, who have clamoured for war, now skulk
into a corner the moment war is about to be declared?
Shall we, who for so many years have been tendering our
lives and fortunes to the general goverment, now come out
with evasions and pitifull excuses the moment tender is
accepted?

But another and a nobler feeling should impell us to
action. *Who are we? and for what are we going to fight?*
are we the titled Slaves of George the third? the military
conscripts of Napolon the great? or the frozen peasants of
the Rusian Czar? No—we are the free born sons of america; the citizens of the only republick now existing in the
world; and the only people on earth who possess rights,
liberties, and property which the[y] dare call their own.

For what are we going to fight? To satisfy the revenge
or ambition of a corrupt and infatuated ministry? to place
another and another diadem on the head of an apostate republican general? to settle the ballance of power among
an assasin tribe of Kings and emperors? "or to preserve to
the prince of Blood, and the grand dignitaries of the empire" their overgrown wealth and exclusive privileges? No:
Such splendid atchievements as these can form no part of
the objects of an american war. But we are going to fight
for the re-establishment of our national charector, misunderstood and vilified at home and abroad; for the protection of our maritime citizens, impressed on board British
ships of war and compelled to fight the battles of our enemies against ourselves; to vindicate our right to a free
trade, and open a market for the productions of our soil,
now perishing on our hands because the *mistress of the
ocean* has forbid us to carry them to any foreign nation; in

fine, to seek some indemnity for past injuries, some security against future aggressions, by the conquest of all the British dominions upon the continent of north america.

Here then is the true and noble principle on which the energies of the nation should be brought into action: *a free people compelled to reclaim by the power of their arms the right which god has bestowed upon them, and which an infatuated King has said they shall not enjoy.*

In such a contest will the people shrink from the support of their goverment; or rather will the[y] shrink from the support of themselves? Will the[y] abandon their great unprescriptible rights, and tamely surrender that illustrious national charector which was purchased with so much blood in the war of the Revolution? No. Such infamy shall not fall upon us. The advocates of Kingly power shall not enjoy the triumph of seeing a free people desert themselves, and crouch before the slaves of a foreign tyrant. The patriotic tender of voluntary service of the invincible grays Capt. F. Stumps independant company and a correspondent display of patriotism by the voluntary tender of service from the counties of Davidson Sumner Smith and Rutherford, is a sure pledge that the free sons of the west will never *submit to such degradation.*

But the period of youth is the season for martial exploits; and accordingly it is upon the young men of america that the eye of the nation is now fixed. They in a peculiar degree are the proper subjects of a volunteer expedition. To say nothing of the generous courage which distinguishes that period of life, they, from their particular situation, can quit their homes at the shortest notice with the least inconvenience to themselves. Unencumbered with families and free from the embarrassment of domestic concerns they are ready at a moments warning to march to any extremity of the republick.

Should the occupation of the canadas be resolved upon by the general goverment, how pleasing the prospect that would open to the young volunteer, while performing a military *promenade* into a distant country, a succession of new and interesting objects would perpetually fill and delight his imagination the effect of which would be heightened by the war like appearence, the martial music, and the grand evolutions of an army of fifty thousand men.

To view the stupendous works of nature, exemplified in the falls of Niagara and the cataract of Montmorenci; to tread the consecrated spot on which Wolf and Montgomery fell, would of themselves repay the young soldier for a march across the continent. But why should these inducements be held out to the young men of america? They need them not. Animated as they are by an ambition to rival the exploits of Rome, they will never prefer an inglorious sloth, a supine inactivity to the honourable toil of carrying the republican standard to the heights of abraham.

In consideration of all which and to carry into effect the object of the general goverment in demanding a voluntary force, to give to the valiant young men of the second military Division of the state of Tennessee an opportunity to evince their devoted affection to the service of the republick; the Major General of the said division has thereupon ordered

1 That the militia of the second military division of the state of Tennessee be forthwith mustered by the proper officers.

2 That the act of congress for raising a volunteer corps of 50,000 men be read at the head of each company.

3 That all persons willing to volunteer under the said act be immediately *enrolled* formed into companies, officered, and reported to the Major Genl.

4 The Generals of Brigade, attached to the second division are charged with the prompt execution of these orders.

March 7, 1812.

III. "The *Carnage* Was *Dreadfull*"

Jackson won his first notable military engagement on March 27, 1814, when as a major general of the United States Volunteers he commanded the troops that defeated the Creek Indians at Tohopeka (Horseshoe Bend) in the present state of Alabama. Five days later he wrote his wife this account of the battle.

To Mrs. Jackson*

Headquarters, Fort Williams

April 1st, 1814

My Dear, I returned to this place on yesterday three oclock p.m. from an excursion against Tohopeka, and about one hour after had the pleasure of receiving your affectionate letter of the 22nd. ultimo.

I have the pleasure to state to you that on the 27th march

---

* From the microfilm collection of the Jackson MSS. in Butler Library, Columbia University. The original of this letter is in the Jackson MSS. in the Library of Congress.

that I attacked & have destroyed the whole combined force, of the Newyokas, oakfuskas, Hillabays, Fish ponds, acacas, and ufalee, Tribes. The *carnage* was *dreadfull*. They had possessed themselves of one of the most military sites, I ever saw, which they had as strongly fortified with logs, across the neck of a bend. I endeavored, to level the works with my cannon, but in vain. The balls passed thro the works without shaking the wall, but carrying destruction to the enemy behind it. I had sent Genl Coffee across the river, with his horse and Indians who had compleatly surrounded the bend, which cut off their escape, and the cherokees effected a landing on the extreme point of the bend with about one hundred and fifty of Genls Coffees Brigade, including Capt Russles spy company. The Battle raged, about two hours, when I found those engaged in the interior of the bend, were about to be overpowered, I ordered, the charge and carried the works, by storm—after which they Indians took possession of the river bank, and part of their works raised with brush getting into the interior of the bend—and it was dark before we finished killing them. I ordered the dead bodies of the Indians to be counted, the next morning, and exclusive of those buried in their watry grave, who were killed in the [water] and who after being wounded plunged into it, there were counted, five hundred and fifty seven. from the report of Genl Coffee and the officers surrounding the bend, they are of oppinion, that there could not be less than three hundred, killed in the river, who sunk and could not be counted. I have no doubt, but at least Eight hundred and fifty were slain—about twenty who had hid under the bank in the water, made their Escape in the night, one of whom was taken the next morning who gives this account, that they were all wounded from which I believe about 19 wounded Indians alone escaped. We took about three hundred and fifty prisoners, weoman & children and three warriors. What effect this will produce upon those infatuated and deluded people I cannot yet say—having destroyed at Tohopeka, three of their principl prophets leaving but two in their nation—having tread their holy ground as the[y] termed it, and destroyed all their chiefs & warriors on the Tallapoosee river above the big bend, it is probable they may now sue for peace Should they not (If I can be supplied with provisions) I will give them, with the permission of heaven the final stroke at the hickory ground, in a few days we have lost in killed of the whites 26, and one hundred and seven wounded. amongst the former is Major Montgomery who bravely fell on the walls, and of the latter Colo. Carroll, slightly—our friends all safe, and Jack you may say to Mrs. Caffery reallised all my expectations he fought bravely, and killed an indian—every officer and man did his duty—the 39th. distinguished themselves and so did the militia, who stormed the works with them. there never was more heroism or roman courage displayed—I write in haste surrounded with a pressure of business, and a little fatigued. I will write you again before I leave this place. For the present I can only add, that I hope shortly to put an end to the war and return to your arms, kiss my little andrew for me, tell him I have a warriors bow & quiver for him. Give my compliments to all friends, and cheer up the spirits of your sister cafferry, and receive my sincere prayers for your health & happiness untill I return. affectionately adieu.

IV. "*More* Could Not Have Been Expected from Veterans Inured to War"

On the day after his famous victory over the British at New Orleans, Jackson wrote the following report of the battle to Secretary of War James Monroe.

*To Secretary Monroe**

Camp 4 miles below [New] Orleans, 9th Jan. 1815

Sir—During the days of the 6th and 7th, the enemy had been actively employed in making preparations for an attack on my lines. With infinite labor they had succeeded on the night of the 7th in getting their boats across from the lake to the river, by widening and deepening the canal on which they had effected their disembarkation. It had not been in my power to impede these operations by a general attack: added to other reasons, the nature of the troops under my command, mostly militia, rendered it too hazardous to attempt extensive *offensive* movements in an open country, against a numerous and well disciplined army. Although my forces, as to number, had been increased by the arrival of the Kentucky division, my strength had received very little addition; a small portion only of that detachment being provided with arms. Compelled thus to wait the attack of the enemy, I took every measure to repel it when it should be made, and to defeat the object he had in view. General Morgan, with the New Orleans contingent, the Louisiana militia and a strong detachment

---

* Reprinted from *Niles' Weekly Register*, VII (February 11, 1815), p. 373.

of the Kentucky troops, occupied an entrenched camp on the opposite side of the river, protected by strong batteries on the bank, erected and superintended by commodore Patterson.

In *my* encampment every thing was ready for action, when, early on the morning of the 8th, the enemy after throwing a heavy shower of bombs and Congreve rockets, advanced their columns on my right and left, to storm my entrenchments. I cannot speak sufficiently in praise of the firmness and deliberation with which my whole line received their approach—*more* could not have been expected from veterans inured to war. For an hour the fire of the small arms was as incessant and severe as can be imagined. The artillery, too, directed by officers who displayed equal skill and courage, did great execution. Yet the columns of the enemy continued to advance with a firmness which reflects upon them the greatest credit. Twice the column which approached me on my left, was repulsed by the troops of General Carroll, those of General Coffee, and a division of the Kentucky militia, and twice they formed again and renewed the assault. At length, however, cut to pieces, they fled in confusion from the field, leaving it covered with their dead and wounded. The loss which the enemy sustained on this occasion, cannot be estimated at less than 1500 in killed, wounded and prisoners. Upwards of three hundred have already been delivered over for burial; and my men are still engaged in picking them up within my lines and carrying them to the point where the enemy are to receive them. This is in addition to the dead and wounded whom the enemy have been enabled to carry from the field, during and since the

action, and to those who have since died of the wounds
they received. We have taken about 500 prisoners, upwards of 300 of whom are wounded, and a great part of
them mortally. My loss has not exceeded, and I believe
has not amounted to ten killed and as many wounded. The
entire destruction of the enemy's army was now inevitable,
had it not been for an unfortunate occurrence which at this
moment took place on the other side of the river. Simul-
taneously with his advance, upon my lines, he had thrown
over in his boats a considerable force to the other side of
the river. *These* having landed were hardy enough to advance against the works of general Morgan; and what is
strange and difficult to account for, at the very moment
when their entire discomfiture was looked for with a confidence approaching to certainty, the Kentucky reinforcements, ingloriously fled, drawing after them, by their
example, the remainder of the forces; and thus yielding
to the enemy that most fortunate position. The batteries
which had rendered me, for many days, the most important service, though bravely defended, were of course now
abandoned; not however, until the guns had been spiked.

This unfortunate route had totally changed the aspect
of affairs. The enemy now occupied a position from which
they might annoy us without hazard, and by means of
which they might have been enabled to defeat, in a great
measure, the effects of our success on this side the river.
It became therefore an object of the first consequence to
dislodge him as soon as possible. For this object, all the
means in my power, which I could with safety use, were
immediately put in preparation. Perhaps, however, it was
somewhat owing to another cause that I succeeded beyond

my expectations. In negociating the terms of a temporary suspension of hostilities to enable the enemy to bury their dead and provide for their wounded, I had required certain propositions to be acceded to as a basis; among which was this one—that although hostilities should cease on *this* side the river until 12 o'clock of this day, yet it was not to be understood that they should cease on the *other* side; but that no reinforcements should be sent across by *either* army until the expiration of that day. His excellency major-general Lambert begged time to consider of these propositions until 10 o'clock of to-day, and in the meantime re-crossed his troops. I need not tell you with how much eagreness I immediately regained possession of the position he had thus hastily quitted.

The enemy having concentered his forces, may again attempt to drive me from my position by storm. Whenever he *does*, I have no doubt my men will act with their usual firmness, and sustain a character now become dear to them.

I have the honor to be,

With great respect,

Your obedient servant

V. "Self Defence Justified Me in Every Act I Did"

JACKSON's active military career ended with the Florida campaign, which he undertook more or less on his own initiative because of Spain's refusal or inability to prevent the Indians and ex-slaves in its province from raiding settlements in the United States. Jackson's account of his exploits in Florida is contained in this letter to George W. Campbell, the United States Minister to Russia.

To George W. Campbell*

Chekisaw Nation, Treaty Ground, October 5, 1818

... On the subject of my taking Pensacola, I regret that the Government, had not furnished you with a copy of my report from Fts. Gadsden and Montgomery, this would have given you a full view of the whole Ground. you are advised of the situation of our Southern frontier, when I was ordered to take the field and "put a speedy end to the conflict with the Seminoles" etc etc. our frontier when I reached it was reeking with the blood of our women and children, and the masacre of Ft Scott. when I reached Ft Scott I found it out of supplies, and no alternative left me, but to abandon the campaign or to force my way to the bay of Appelachecola, and risque meeting supplies I had ordered from N. Orleans I choose the latter—and succeeded— having obtained eight days rations for my men I immediately marched on Mickasookey where the strength of the enemy was collected, first apprising the Govr. of Pensacola the reason why I had entered the floridas, to wit, not as the enemy but as the friend of Spain, as Spain had acknowledged her incapacity through her weakness to control the Indians within her territory and keep them at peace with the United States. Self Defence justified our entering her

* Reprinted from John Spencer Bassett, ed., *Correspondence of Andrew Jackson* (Washington, 1926-1935), Vol. II, pp. 395-398. Reprinted with the permission of the Carnegie Institution of Washington. The original of this letter is in the St. Louis Mercantile Library.

Territory, and doing that for her which she had bound herself to do by solem Treaty. that as I was engaged fighting the Battles of Spain, I had a right, and did calculate on receiving all the facilities in the power of the agents of Spain, that would aid me in putting a speedy end to the war, advising the Governor in the same letter that I had ordered supplies up the Escambia for my army to Ft Crawford, which I trusted would be permitted to pass unmolested, and without any delay occasioned by the agents of Spain. but should I be disappointed in my expectations of the friendly disposition of the agents of Spain, or should my supplies be interrupted by them, I should view it as an act of war and treat it accordingly.

I recd an answer to this friendly letter, a positive declaration that my provisions should not pass, the supplies were by the Governor seized at Pensacola under a demand of Transit duties, and my whole army thereby made subject to starvation, and which I never got untill I entered Pensacola. I proceeded against Mickasookey routed and dispersed the enemy, Taking some prisoners from whom I learned, that the Indians recd all their supplies of ammunition from St Marks thirty miles distant, that the noted and notorious villain—Francis the prophet and his party had retired to St Marks with all his Booty taken from Ft Scott and McQueen and his party had retired there also, that the ballance of the Indians had fled to the Negroes on the Suwaney river, I was also informed by the Governor of Pensacola, through Captains Call and Gordon, that he expected St Marks was in the hands of the Indians and Negroes, as they had made demand of large supplies, which the commandant was not able to comply with, and he was unable to defend the Fort as soon as I had collected

the corn and cattle for the supply of my Troops, I marched
on St Marks When I reached there I found, that Francis
and party had been in the Ft, that the garrison had been
supplied with the cattle stolen from our frontier, that the
Public stores were the granaries of our enemy, and that
the Indians had been supplied with all kind of munitions
of war by the Commandant, and that the notorious Arbuthnot was then in the garrison. I demanded possession of
the garrison, to be possessed by my Troops during the war
and untill Spain could reinforce it with as many troops as
would insure the safety of our frontier and a fullfilment of
the Treaty with the U. States on the part of Spain, this was
refused me. I saw across St Marks river the smoke of my
enemy delay was out of the Question, I seized Arbuthnot
in the garrison and took possession of it. The noted Francis,
who had just returned with a Brigadier Genl commission,
a good Rifle and snuf box presented by the Prince Regent
had been captured the day before with four of his followers, by Capt McKeever whose vessell they had vissitted,
mistaking it for a vessell expected from england with supplies for the Indians as he stated. I ordered him and his
principle chief to be hung, and marched the next day for
Suwaney where I routed the Indians and Negroes, Took
Ambrister a British officer, who headed the Negroes [and]
Arbuthnots Schooner, with all their papers which led to
the conviction and execution of Arbuthnot and Capt Ambrister both of whom was executed under Sentence of a
court martial at St Marks.

I returned to Ft Gadsden when proposing to disband
the militia force, I recd information that five hundred and
fifty Indians had collected in Pensacola, was fed by the

Governor, and a party furnished by the Govr had Issued
forth and in one night slaughtered eighteen of our citizens, and that another party had with the knowledge of
the Governor and being furnished by him went out publickly, murdered a Mr. Stockes and family and had in open
day returned to Pensacola and sold the Booty amongst
which was the cloathing of Mrs Stokes. This Statement
was corroborated by a report of Gov. Bibb, I was also informed that the provisions I had ordered for the supply of
Ft Crawford and my army on board the U States Schooner
Amelia was seized and delivered at Pensacola. With a small
detachment of regulars and six hundred Tennesseans I
marched from Pensacola, whilst on my march thither I was
met by a protest of the Governor of Pensacola, ordering
me out of the Floridas, or he would oppose force, to force
and drive me out of the Territory of Spain This bold Measure of the Governor, who had alledged weakness as the
cause of his non fulfilment of the treaty with the U States,
when united with the facts stated, and which then I had
positive proof, that at that time a large number of the hostile Indians were then in Pensacola who I had dispersed
East of the Apelachecola unmasked the duplicity of the
Governor and his having aided and abetted the Indians in
the war against us, I hastened my steps, entered Pensacola,
Took possession of my supplies—the Governor had fled
from the city to the Barancos, where he had strongly fortified himself. I demanded possession of the garrison to be
held by American Troops untill a gurantee should be given
for the fullfilment of the treaty and the safety of the frontier, this was denied. I approached the Barancos with one
9 lb. peace and 5, 8/10 Inch howitzer, the[y] opened their

batteries upon me it was returned spiritedly, and with two
pieces against forty odd mounted of 24 down, the white
flag went up in the Evening and the capitulation entered
into which you have seen This time I had my ladders ready
to go over the wall, which I believe the garrison discovered,
and was afraid of a night attack and surrendered, When
the flag was hoisted the[y] had three hundred effectives
in the garrison. This number of americans could have kept
it from combined Urope There was one Indian wounded
in the garrison, and the others were sent out in the night
across the bay before I got possession.

Thus Sir I have given you a concise statement of the
facts, and all I regret is that I had not stormed the works
captured the Gov. put him on his trial for the murder of
Stokes and his family and hung him for the Deed I could
adopt no other way to *"put an end to the war"* but by possessing myself of the strong hold that was an asylum to the
enemy, afforded them the means of offence, the officers of
Spain having by their acts Identified themselves with our
enemy, become such, and by the law of nations subjected
themselves to be treated as such. self Defence justified me
in every act I did, I will stand justified before god and all
urope and I regret that our government, has extended the
courtesy to Spain of withdrawing the troops from Pensacola before Spain gave a gurantee for the fulfilment of the
Treaty and the safety of our frontier, it was an act of courtesy that nothing but the insignificance and weakness of
Spain can excuse but it is not my province to find fault
with the acts of the government; but it may have reason to
repent of her clemency.

Make a tender to your lady of my sincere respects and

best wishes for her happiness and reserve for yourself an expression of my unfeigned friendship and Esteem and remain respectfully

yr mo. ob. serv.

P.S. My eyes are weak and my hand trembles—I am still weak and much debilitated, nothing but the hope of being serviceable to the wishes of my Government and the interest of the state of Tennessee could have induced me to have undertaken the journey—A.J.

II • The Appeal to the People

I. "THE FREE WILL OF THOSE WHO HAVE ALONE THE RIGHT TO DECIDE"

WHEN Jackson was nominated as a candidate for the Presidency by the Tennessee legislature in July 1822, he wrote: "I have never been a candidate for any office. I never will. But the people have a right to choose whom the[y] will to perform their constitutional duties, and when the people call, the Citizen is bound to render the service required." In February 1823 he again explained his position in a letter to H. W. Peterson, who had informed Jackson that he had been unanimously nominated for the Presidency by a group of citizens meeting in Harrisburg, Pennsylvania.

To H. W. Peterson*

Nashville, 23 Feb. 1823

Sir, Your letter of the 3d instant, with the Harrisburgh paper entitled the Commonwealth, containing the address you have alluded to, has been this day received. The complimentary manner in which my fellow citizens of Pennsyl-

---

* From the microfilm collection of the Jackson MSS. in Butler Library, Columbia University. The original of this letter is in the Jackson MSS. in the Library of Congress.

vania have been pleased to notice my military services, & their voluntary expressions of respect & confidence in me, has excited in me a proper sense of gratitude.

As a member of a Committee appointed to draft an address to the People of the U S on the subject of the next Presidential election, *and by the request of that Committee* you ask to be informed "whether I can or do approve of" my name being use at this time as a candidate "for the Presidency of the U States."

I should have consulted my own feelings by continuing to avoid speaking on the subject but the respectable source from whence the inquiry emanates, prohibits any but a candid notice of your communication.

My undeviating rule of conduct through life, and which I have & shall ever deem as congenial with true Republican principles of government, has been never to seek, or decline public invitations to office. For the services which I may have rendered & which have, it is hoped, proved in a degree beneficial to my country I have nothing to ask. They have been richly repaid with the confidence & good opinion of the virtuous and well deserving part of the community. I have only essayed to discharge a debt which every man owes his country when her rights are invaded; and if twelve years exposure to fatigue & numerous privations can warrant the expression: I may venture to assert that my portion of public service has been performed & that with this impression I had retired from the busy scenes of public life: with a desire to be a spectator merely of passing events.

The office of Chief Magistrate of the Union is one of great responsibility; as it should not be sought by any Individual of the Republic: so it cannot with propriety be declined when offered by those who have the power of selection. It is interresting to the American People alone & in the election they should exercise their free and unbiased judgement. It was with these impressions I presume & without any consultation with me, that the Members of the Legislature of the State of Tennessee as an additional testimony of their confidence in me: thought proper to present my name to the consideration of the American community. My political creed prompts me to leave the affair uninfluenced by an expression on my part: & to the free will of those who have alone the right to decide.

II. "A Careful and Judicious Tariff Is Much Wanted"

ALTHOUGH Jackson refused to campaign for the Presidency in 1824, he did announce his stand on the tariff. The following letter, which contains his only discussion of any of the issues of the campaign of 1824, reveals that he was a skillful politician who knew how to appeal to virtually every segment of the American electorate.

To L. H. Coleman*

Washington city, April 26th, 1824

Sir: I have had the honor, this day, to receive your letter of the 21st instant, and, with candor, shall reply to it. My name has been brought before the nation by the people themselves, without any agency of mine; for I wish it not

---

* Reprinted from *Niles' Weekly Register*, XXVI (June 12, 1824), p. 245.

to be forgotten that I have never solicited office; nor, when called upon by the constituted authorities, have ever declined, where I conceived my services would be beneficial to my country. But, as my name had been brought before the nation for the first office in the gift of the people, it is incumbent on me, when asked, frankly to declare my opinion upon any political [or] national question, pending before, and about which the country feels an interest.

You ask me my opinion on the tariff. I answer, that I am in favor of a judicious examination and revision of it; and so far as the tariff bill before us embraces the design of fostering, protecting, and preserving within ourselves the means of national defence and independence, particularly in a state of war, I would advocate and support it. The experience of the late war ought to teach us a lesson, and one never to be forgotten. If our liberty and republican form of government, procured for us by our revolutionary fathers, are worth the blood and treasure at which they were obtained, it surely is our duty to protect and defend them. Can there be an American patriot, who saw the privations, dangers, and difficulties experienced for the want of proper means of defence during the last war, who would be willing again to hazard the safety of our country, if embroiled; or to rest it for defence on the precarious means of national resource to be derived from commerce in a state of war with a maritime power, who might destroy that commerce to prevent us obtaining the means of defence, and thereby subdue us? I hope there is not; and if there is, I am sure he does not deserve to enjoy the blessing of freedom. Heaven smiled upon, and gave us liberty and independence. That same Providence has blessed us with the means of national independence and national defence,

If we omit or refuse to use the gifts which he has extended to us, we deserve not the continuation of his blessings. He has filled our mountains and our plains with minerals—with lead, iron and copper; and given us climate and soil for the growing of hemp and wool. These being the grand materials of our national defence, they ought to have extended to them adequate and fair protection, that our own manufactures and laborers may be placed on a fair competition with those of Europe, and that we may have within our own country a supply of those leading and important articles so essential in war. Beyond this, I look at the tariff with an eye to the proper distribution of labor, and to revenue; and with a view to discharge our national debt. I am one of those who do not believe that a national debt is a national blessing, but rather a curse to a republic; inasmuch as it is calculated to raise around the administration a monied aristocracy, dangerous to the liberties of the country. This tariff—I mean a judicious one—possesses more fanciful than real danger. I will ask, what is the real situation of the agriculturalist? Where has the American farmer a market for his surplus product? Except for cotton, he has neither a foreign or home market. Does not this clearly prove, when there is no market either at home or abroad, that there is too much labor employed in agriculture; and that the channels for labor should be multiplied? Common sense points out, at once, the remedy. Draw from agriculture this superabundant labor; employ it in mechanism and manufactures; thereby creating a home market for your bread-stuffs, and distributing labor to a most profitable account; and benefits to the country will result. Take from agriculture in the United States six hundred thousand men, women and children, and you will at once give a home market for more bread-stuffs than all Europe now furnishes us. In short, sir, we have been too long subject to the policy of the British merchants. It is time we should become a little more *Americanized;* and, instead of feeding the paupers and laborers of England, feed our own; or else, in a short time, by continuing our present policy, we shall all be rendered paupers ourselves.

It is, therefore, my opinion that a careful and judicious tariff is much wanted to pay our national debt, and afford us the means of that defence within ourselves, on which the safety of our country and liberty depends; and last, though not least, give a proper distribution to our labor, which must prove beneficial to the happiness, independence and wealth of the community.

This is a short outline of my opinions, generally, on the subject of your inquiry, and believing them correct and calculated to further the prosperity and happiness of my country, I declare to you, I would not barter them for any office or situation of a temporal character, that could be given me.

I have presented you my opinions freely, because I am without concealment; and should, indeed, despise myself, if I could believe myself capable of desiring the confidence of any by means so ignoble.

I am, sir, very respectfully, your most obedient servant,

III. "The Choice of a President Is a Matter for the People"

THIS letter, which was written after the election of 1824 but before the House had given John Quincy Adams a majority of its votes and the Presi-

dency, removes any doubt concerning Jackson's stand
during the preceding campaign and indicates the extent to which he believed in popular rule.

*To Samuel Swartwout**

City of Washington, Dec'br 14th, 1824

Dr Sir, But for the little leisure I have had since my arrival
at this place your letter of the 10th would have been earlier
replied to.

I assure you my dear Sir that so far as my feelings stand
staked on the late contest before the American people, I
feel myself much gratified, and amply remunerated against
everything of unpleasantness which abuse and slander has
heaped upon me, in the recollection and hope that my
friends have been actuated by the purest principles & motives. I recollect with pride & pleasure that in no one instance have I sought by promise or management to draw
to myself the good opinion of a single individual in society;
and that so many should have preferred me to take charge
& administer the affairs of our great & growing country, is
to me a matter of the highest consolation, let the result now
be as it may. There are doubtless many, who might discredit the assertion, tho you will I hope believe it, that upon
this subject I am without any deep concern. I should be
doing injustice to the feelings of those who with such a
zeal & friendship have sustained me in this trial, were I to
assert entire disregard about the matter, nor do I feel a dis-

---

* Reprinted from Henry F. DePuy, "Some Letters of Andrew Jack-
son," *Proceedings of the American Antiquarian Society,* 31 (April 13-
October 19, 1921), pp. 77-79. Reprinted with the permission of the
American Antiquarian Society.

regard particularly when I consider that so many of my
fellow citizens have evinced a preferrence towards me. My
thanks are due to them, and the[y] are most cheerfully extended; yet I do declare to you, that if any favorable result
could be secured thro any intrigue, management, or prom-
ises to be made on my part, I would at once unhesitatingly
& without reserve spurn anything of success. You must not
understand with any other meaning than that which is my
object to convey, it is this; that the choice of a President is
a matter for the people:—to be installed against their will
no man could calculate upon a happy or beneficial administration; neither credit to himself, or advantage to his
country could be the result of his success; & therefore do I
repeat, & assure you that I should feel myself an unhappy,
perhaps degraded man, should anything of management or
arrangement contrary to that consent place me in the Executive chair: a turbulent time will [be] the lot of that
man who may come in thro any channel save that of a
preference by the people; & god grant it may always be so.
To say I have nothing of concern about the office would
be doing injustice to the kind feelings of those who have
sustained me, and would wear the appearance of affecta-
tion; it is my design merely to say, that I would rather remain a plain cultivator of the soil as I am, than to occupy
that which is truly the first office in the world, if the voice
of the nation was against it. With these sentiments I have
lived, and with them I hope to die.

I have toiled for my country, and the advantages she has
derived, I hope, from my services, are to me a pleasing
reflection; and to me it is of higher importance, that our
happiness & plain republican institutions should be well
maintained, than that this or that man shall take charge of

our destinies. I have risqued much for the liberties of our
country, and my anxious & sincere prayer is, that they may
long endure.

Who shall rule is of less importance, than how he may
claim to rule or Govern when in power. . . .

IV. "THE JUDGMENT OF AN ENLIGHTENED
PATRIOTIC & UNCORRUPTED PEOPLE"

WHEN Henry Clay used his influence in the
House of Representatives to make Adams the next
President of the United States, he explained his opposition to Jackson on the ground that he was a "military chieftain." This was a challenge that Jackson
could not ignore, and he replied in a letter that was reprinted in a number of the nation's newspapers.

*To Samuel Swartwout**

Washington City, Fbry 22d, 1825

. . . Yesterday I rec'd your communication adverting to
the reasons and defence presented by Mr. Clay to Judge
Brooks why duty & reflection imposed upon him the necessity of standing in opposition to me, because of my being
as he pleased to style me, "a Military Chieftain." I had
before seen the letter; first when it appeared, I did entertain the opinion, that perhaps some notice of it might be
necessary, for the reason that the expression seemed to
carry with it more the appearance of personality than any

---

* Reprinted from Henry F. DePuy, "Some Letters of Andrew Jackson," *Proceedings of the American Antiquarian Society*, 31 (April 13-
October 19, 1921), pp. 83-86. Reprinted with the permission of the American Antiquarian Society.

thing else; and could the opinion be at all entertained, that it could meet the object, which doubtless was intended, to prejudice me in the estimation of my countrymen, I might yet consider some notice of it necessary; such a belief however I cannot entertain, without insulting the generous testimonial with which by ninety-nine electers of the people I have been honored.

I am well aware that this term "Military Chieftain" has for some time past been a cant phrase with Mr. Clay & certain of his retainers; but the vote with which by the people I have been honored, is enough to satisfy me, that the prejudice by them, sought to be produced availed but little. This sufficient for me. I entertain a deep and heartfelt gratitude to my country, for the confidence & regard she has manifested towards me, leaving to prejudiced minds whatever they can make of the epithet "Military Chieftain."

It is for an ingenuity stronger than mine to conceive what idea was intended to be conveyed by the term. It is very true that early in life, even in the days of boyhood, I contributed my mite to shake off the yoke of tyranny, and to build up the fabrick of free government; and when lately our country was involved in war, having the commission of Major Gen'l of Militia in Tennessee, I made an appeal to the patriotism of the western citizens, when 3000 of them went with me to the field, to support her Eagles. If this can constitute me a "Military Chieftain" I am one. Aided by the patriotism of the western people, and an indulgent providence, it was my good fortune to protect our frontier border from the savages, & successfully to defend an important & vulnerable point of our Union. Our lives were risked, privations endured, sacrafices made, if Mr.

Clay pleases, Martial law declared, not with any view of personal agrandisment, but for the preservation of all and everything that was valuable, the honor safety & glory of our country. Does this constitute a "Military Chieftain"? and are all our brave men in war, who go forth to defend their rights, & the rights of their country to be termed Military Chieftains, and therefor denounced? if so, the tendency of such a doctrine may be, to arrest the ardor of usefull and brave men, in future times of need & peril: with me it shall make no difference; for my country at war I would aid assist & defend her rights, let the consequences to myself be what they might. I have as you very well know, by some of the designing politicians of this country, been charged with taking bold & high-handed measures; but as they were not designed for any benefit to myself I should under similar circumstances not refrain from a course equally bold; that man who in time of difficulty & danger shall halt any course, necessary to maintain the rights & privileges and independence of the country, is unsuited to authority; and if these & sentiments shall entitle me to the name & character of a Military Chieftain I am content so to be considered, satisfied too for Mr. Clay if he chooses, to represent to the citizens of the West, that as the reason why in his opinion I meritted not his & their confidence.

Mr. Clay never yet has risked himself for his country, sacraficed his repose, or made an effort to repel an invading foe; of course his "conscience" assured him that it was altogether wrong in any other man to lead his countrymen to battle & victory. He who fights, and fights successfully must according to his standard be held up as a "Military Chieftain": even Washington could he again appear among us might be so considered, because he dared to be a virtuous and successfull soldier, an honest statesman, & a correct man. It is only when overtaken by disaster & defeat, that any man is to be considered a safe politician & correct statesman.

Defeat might to be sure have brought with it one benefit, it might have enabled me to escape the notice and animadversions of Mr. Clay but considering that by an opposite result, my country has been somewhat benefitted, I rather prefer it even with the opprobrium & censure which he seems disposed to extend. To him thank god I am in no wise responsible, there is a purer tribunal to which in preference I would refer myself—to the Judgment of an enlightened patriotic & uncorrupted people—to that tribunal I would rather appeal whence is derived whatever reputation either he or I are possessed of. By a refference there, it will be ascertained that I did not solicit the office of President, it was the frank & flattering call of the freeman of this country, not mine, which placed my name before the nation; when they failed in their colleges to make a choice, no one beheld me seeking thro art or management to entice any Representative in Congress from a conscientious responsibility to his own, or the wishes of his constituents. No mid-night taper burnt by me; no secret conclaves were held, or cabals entered into, to persuade any to a violation of pledges given, or instructions received. By me no plans were concerted to impair the pure principles of our Republican institutions, or to frustrate that fundamental one which maintains the supremacy of the peoples will; on the contrary, having never in any manner either before the people or Congress in the slightest manner interfered with the question, my conscience stands void of offence, & will

go quietly with me, heedless of the insinuations of any,
who thro management may seek an influence, not sanctioned by merit.

Demagogues I am persuaded have in times past, done
more injury to the cause of freedom & the rights of man,
than ever did a "Military Chieftain,"; and in our country,
at least in times of peace, should be more feared. I have
seen something of this in my march thro life, and have seen
some men too, making the boldest professions who were
more influenced by selfish views & considerations, than
ever they were by any workings of an honest conscience.

I became a soldier for the good of my country: difficulties met me at every step; I thank god it was my good fortune to surmount them. The war over & peace restored I
sought to retire again to my farm, & to private life, where
but for the call made by my country to the Senate I should
have contentedly remained. I never yet been a hanger on
upon office & power, or was willing to hold any post, longer
than I could be usefull to my country, not myself, and I
trust I never shall. If this makes me so, I am a "Military
Chieftain." . . .

V. "An Enquiry for the Succeeding Canvass"

As soon as John Quincy Adams made Henry
Clay Secretary of State, Jackson became convinced
that the two men had entered into a "corrupt bargain"
by which each had helped the other to attain high
office. As the following letter indicates, Jackson was
a good loser, but he was also a man who believed that
he and the people had been cheated.

To Major Henry Lee*

Hermitage, Octr 7th, 1825

. . . I am pleased to read your sentiments with regard to the support due to the administration so far as its measures may redound to the prosperity of our common country. Mr Adams is the Constitutional President and as such I would myself be the last man in the Commonwealth to oppose him upon any other ground than that of principle. How he reached the office is an enquiry for the succeeding canvass, when the principles of the constitution, apart from his ministerial acts, or at least without necessary opposition to them, will sanction the investigation. As to his character also, it is hardly necessary for me to observe, that I had esteemed him as a virtuous, able and honest man; and when rumor was stamping the sudden union of his and the friends of Mr Clay with intrigue, barter and bargain, I did not, nay, I could not believe that Mr Adams participated in a management deserving such epithets. Accordingly when the election was terminated, I manifested publicly a continuation of the same high opinion of his virtue, and of course my disbelief of his having had knowledge of the pledges, which many men of high standing boldly asserted to be the price of his election. But when these strange rumors became facts, when the predicted stipulation was promptly fulfilled, and Mr Clay was Secretary of State, the inferrence was irresistible. I could not doubt the facts. It was well known that during the canvass Mr Clay had denounced him as an apostate, as one of the most dangerous

---

* From the microfilm collection of the Jackson MSS. in Butler Library, Columbia University. The original of this letter is in the Jackson MSS. in the Library of Congress.

men in the union, and the last men in it that ought to be brought into the executive chair. . . . I do not think the human mind can resist the conviction that the whole prediction was true, and that Mr Adams by the redemption of the pledge stood at once before the American people as a participant in the disgraceful traffic of Congressional votes for executive office. From that moment I withdrew all intercourse with him, not however to oppose his administration when I think it useful to the country,—here feeble as my aid may be it will always be freely given. But I withdrew in accordance with another principle not at all in conflict with such a course. It is that which regulating the morals of society, to superior office would invite *virtue unrespected,* and in the private relations of life forbids an association with those whom we believe corrupt or capable of cherishing vice when it ministers to selfish aggrandisement. . . .

VI. "I WILL NOT *Abandon Principle* TO SECURE TO MYSELF THE HIGHEST *Boon*"

IN OCTOBER 1825 the Tennessee legislature again nominated Jackson for the Presidency. Although his managers conducted an intensive campaign that culminated in his victory in 1828, Jackson did nothing to promote his candidacy. In this letter, which was written a short time before his election, he explains once again why he would neither seek nor refuse the Presidency.

To Richard M. Johnson*

[Hermitage] September, 1828

. . . Had you my Dr. sir reflected that I am not a candidate for the presidency by my own volition, but by the selection of the people, you would not for a moment entertain the idea, that it would be proper for me now to adopt the electioneering course pursued by our travelling cabinet. I have long since announced my principles to the nation and in pursuance of them have been silent amidst the violent torrents of the vilest calumny ever heaped upon man, leaving to the virtue of the people my Justification. Being thus brought out by the people, it is for them without any agency of mine to sustain me, for I will not *abandon principle* to secure to myself the highest *Boon*.

When we see a travelling cabinet ranging over the continent, wielding its patronage for the purpose of corrupting the elective franchise and thereby inflicting a wound on our national character not easily to be washed out, it behoves me at least, to shew by my acts that the professions I have made were based upon principle, & that I will not depart from *them*. My enemies would delight to see me *now* entering upon an electioneering tour. It would realise the saying ascribed to Mr Adams, "that he would turn democrat & urge them into such extravagance that the whole people would become disgusted with our government, & cry out for a change." The people having taken me up must determine the canvass themselves, without any agency of mine. If they succeed, than it can with truth be

---

* From the microfilm collection of the Jackson MSS. in Butler Library, Columbia University. The original of this letter is in the Jackson MSS. in the Library of Congress.

said, that virtue has triumphed over the corrupting influence of executive patronage & designing Demagogues. *The people must themselves Triumph*—a great principle is at stake, & if they do, then it can be said all power flows from them, & when their agents violate their declared will, they will be hurled from their confidence. Then will our Republican form of government endure forever, but if the dictation of designing demagogues be acknowledged, freedom & independence are gone. I do not despair of the republic. . . .

III • The Spoils of Reform

I. "The Manifest Will of the People"

Although Jackson in 1798 condemned John Adams for "removing all those from office who differ with him in politicks," he used much the same system during his own administration. On the other hand, it should be remembered that Jackson's role as a spoils politician has usually been exaggerated, that he wished to make the nation's civil servants responsible to the majority, and that he always looked on rotation in office as a "reform." Just how Jackson intended to reform the Federal bureaucracy is revealed by the "Outline of Principles" which he prepared a few days before his first inauguration.

Outline of Principles Submitted to the Heads of Department*

Febr. 23d. 1829

The late political struggle exhibited the people acting against an improper use of the patronage in the hands of the executive branch of the General Govt. A patronage whose tendency was a corruption of the elective franchise,

* From the microfilm collection of the Jackson MSS. in Butler Library, Columbia University. The original of this memorandum is in the Jackson MSS. in the Library of Congress.

in as much as it sought to mould the public sentiment into
an acquiesence with the exercise of power acquired without the sanction of that sentiment. It follows as a consequence, that the president of the people is to reform the
abuses of which they complained, and repair, as far as he
can, the individual and public injury produced by them.
and that it becomes his duty in conformity with this principle to dismiss all officers who were appointed against the
manifest will of the people, or whose official station by a
subserviency to selfish electioneering purposes was made
to operate against the freedom of state elections.

The same principle will also require of any Head of Depart., a strict examination into the state of his Dept, and a
report to the President, stating what retrenchments can be
made without injury to the public service, what offices can
be dispensed with, and what improvement made in the
economy and dispatch of business.

Connected with the character of the administration are
the moral habits of those who may be entrusted with its
various subordinate duties. Officers in their private and
public relations should be examples of fidelity & honesty;
otherwise the interests of the community will require their
removal, and they will have to be removed. A strict adherence to this rule will increase the scope of the rotative
principle in office, and contribute in this respect to elevate
the character of the government, and purify the morals of
the country. This principle will be regarded as a fundamental one by the President, and as the best check for the
evils arising out of the growing propensity for office.

II. "MY FEELINGS HAVE BEEN SEVERELY CORRODED"

DURING the first months of his administration Jackson had to listen to countless hard-luck stories from applicants for positions in the Federal government. Reform may have been desirable, but in practice it could also be heartrending; and the President was often in the anomalous position of sponsoring a reduction in the number of government clerks while at the same time using his own funds to aid the families of disappointed office seekers.

To Rev. Hardy M. Cryer*

Washington, May 16, 1829

My D'r Sir, Your kind letter of the 20th ult, has been some days before me. The great press of business has prevented me from attending to it sooner, and even now I can only say to you as it regards our mutual friend Mr Gwinn that he had better remain where he is, untill you hear from me again. There is more distressed people here, than any person could imagine who were not an eye witness to the various applications for relief. My feelings have been severely corroded by the various applications for relief, and as far as real charitable objects presented themselves, I have yielded my might to their relief. would you believe it, that a lady who had once rolled in wealth, but whose husband was overtaken by misfortune and reduced to want, and

* Reprinted from Bassett, *Correspondence of Andrew Jackson,* Vol. IV, p. 33. Reprinted with the permission of the Carnegie Institution of Washington. The original of this letter is in the Tennessee Historical Society.

is, and has been an applicant for office, and well recommended, applied to me with tears in her eyes, soliciting
relief, assuring me that her children were starving, and to
buy them a morsel of bread she had to sell her thimble the
day before. an office I had not to give, and my cash [?]
was nearly out, but I could not withhold from her half of
the pittance I had with me. I name these things to bring
to your view that from the extravagance of this place how
small a prospect is $1000 per annum for the support of a
family here, and the moment they are out of office, starvation presents itself to view.

We have not had leisure yet, to make the necessary arrangements of reform—we are progressing, and such is the
press for office, and the distress here that there are for the
place of. messenger (for the Departments) at least twenty
applicants for each station, and many applicants who have
been men of wealth and respectability. still if our friend
Gwinn wishes to come on here, when we finally organise
the Departments, and turn out the spies from our camp,
I will preserve an office for him, but we are now having a
thorough investigation of all Departments, and the enquiry will be made how many, if any clerks, can be dispensed with. . . .

III. "Offices Are Created Solely for the Benefit of the People"

In this excerpt from his first annual message
Jackson explains why in his opinion rotation in office
is an essential feature of democratic government and
why "no one man has any more intrinsic right to official
station than another."

Message*

December 8, 1829

Fellow-Citizens of the Senate and House of Representatives:

. . . There are perhaps few men who can for any great length of time enjoy office and power, without being more or less under the influence of feelings unfavorable to the faithful discharge of their public duties. Their integrity may be proof against improper considerations immediately addressed to themselves; but they are apt to acquire a habit of looking with indifference upon the public interests, and of tolerating conduct from which an unpracticed man would revolt. Office is considered as a species of property; and Government rather as a means of promoting individual interests than as an instrument created solely for the service of the People. Corruption in some and in others a perversion of correct feelings and principles divert Government from its legitimate ends, and make it an engine for the support of the few at the expense of the many. The duties of all public officers are, or at least admit of being made, so plain and simple that men of intelligence may readily qualify themselves for their performance; and I cannot but believe that more is lost by the long continuance of men in office than is generally to be gained by their experience. I submit, therefore, to your consideration whether the efficiency of the Government would not be promoted and official industry and integrity better secured

---

* Reprinted from *Senate Documents*, 21 Congress, 1 Session, 1829-1830, Vol. I, Doc. No. 1, p. 8.

by a general extension of the law which limits appointments to four years.

In a country where offices are created solely for the benefit of the people no one man has any more intrinsic right to official station than another. Offices were not established to give support to particular men at the public expense. No individual wrong is, therefore, done by removal, since neither appointment to nor continuance in office is matter of right. The incumbent became an officer with a view to public benefits; and when these require his removal they are not to be sacrificed to private interests. It is the People, and they alone, who have a right to complain when a bad officer is substituted for a good one. He who is removed has the same means of obtaining a living that are enjoyed by the millions who never held office. The proposed limitation would destroy the idea of property now so generally connected with official station; and although individual distress may be sometimes produced, it would, by promoting that rotation which constitutes a leading principle in the republican creed, give healthful action to the system. . . .

Andrew Jackson

IV. "An Honorable Testimonial for My Administration"

Historians with few exceptions have written about Jackson's handling of the patronage from his opponents' rather than from his point of view. Thus, while it is generally asserted that the spoils system made possible the creation of a powerful Democratic party machine during his Administration, Jackson in this letter maintains that his management of the Federal bureaucracy aroused the hostility rather than "the affection of the office Holders."

*To Joseph Conn Guild**

Wash., April 24, 1835

... I perceive among other artifices employed by those late adherents of the administration, who have turned against it, that it is now pretended that my policy is sustained, by the corrupt office holders! The truth is, the people have always sustained me both against the majority of the office holders, of the politicians, & the public presses of the country. I have long since perceived that no administration will ever command the affection of the office Holders which seeks to extirpate abuses & which acknowledges the right of the people to reach through the election of the Chief Executive, every subordinate officer, & thus to remove all who shall have given dissatisfaction to the public. The mass of the Office Holders, will always cling to that party which would establish a life estate in office, give high salaries & exact small service. This party is the aristocracy & hence it is, that the Democratic party has, (although in the ascendancy for the greatest part of the time since the establishment of the Government) always been in the minority in the official corps. For the most part whenever a man obtains station, he adopts those principles calculated to make it lucrative & permanent—he grows jealous of the power of the people, which makes or seems to render his

---

* From the microfilm collection of the Jackson MSS. in Butler Library, Columbia University. The original of this letter is in the Jackson MSS. in the Library of Congress.

situation precarious, & imperceptibly & gradually all his feelings & political biases are surrendered to the leading men who would make Government in its great & minor officers independent altogether of the people. I consider it, therefore, an honorable testimonial for my administration, that I have been harassed by the clamor of officeholders from the beginning up to this hour. . . .

IV · The Sanctity of
the Union

I. "The Union Will Be Preserved"

As soon as Jackson learned that a South Carolina convention had adopted an ordinance nullifying
the tariffs of 1828 and 1832, he took steps to crush what
he considered "positive treason." In this letter to the
leader of the Unionists in South Carolina, he makes
clear his willingness to resort to force to uphold the
Union.

To Joel R. Poinsett*

Washington, December 9, 1832

My D'r Sir, Your letters were this moment recd, from the
hands of Col. Drayton, read and duly considered, and in
haste I reply. The true spirit of patriotism that they breath
fills me with pleasure. If the Union party unite with you,
heart and hand in the text you have laid down, you will
not only preserve the union, but save our native state, from
that ruin and disgrace into which her treasonable leaders
have attempted to plunge her. All the means in my power,

---

* Reprinted from Bassett, *Correspondence of Andrew Jackson*, Vol.
IV, pp. 497-498. Reprinted with the permission of the Carnegie Institution of Washington. The original of this letter is in the Historical Society
of Pennsylvania.

I will employ to enable her own citizens, those faithful patriots, who cling to the Union to put it down.

The proclamation I have this day Issued, and which I inclose you, will give you my views, of the treasonable conduct of the convention and the Governors recommendation to the assembly—it is not merely rebellion, but the act of raising troops, positive treason, and I am assured by all the members of congress with whom I have conversed that I will be sustained by congress. If so, I will meet it at the threshold, and have the leaders arrested and arraigned for treason—I am only waiting to be furnished with the acts of your Legislature, to make a communication to Congress, ask the means necessary to carry my proclamation into compleat affect, and by an exemplary punishment of those leaders for treason so unprovoked, put down this rebellion, and strengthen our happy government both at home and abroad.

My former letter and the communication from the Dept. of War, will have informed you of the arms and equipments having been laid in Deposit subject to your requisition, to aid the civil authority in the due execution of the law, *whenever called on as the posse comitatus,* etc. etc.

The vain threats of resistance by those who have raised the standard of rebellion shew their madness and folly. You may assure those patriots who cling to their country, and this union, which alone secures our liberty prosperity and happiness, that in forty days, I can have within the limits of So. Carolina fifty thousand men, and in forty days more another fifty thousand—However potant the threat of resistance with only a population of 250,000 whites and nearly that double in blacks with our ships in the port to aid in the execution of our laws?—The wickedness, madness and folly of the leaders and the delusion of their followers in the attempt to destroy themselves and our union has not its paralel in the history of the world. The Union will be preserved, The safety of the republic, the supreme law, which will be promptly obeyed by me.

I will be happy to hear from you often thro' Col. Mason or his son, if you think the postoffice unsafe I am with sincere respect

yr mo. obdt. servt.

II. "Your Sacred Union"

The "Proclamation," which was written by Secretary of State Edward Livingston and issued by Jackson on December 10, 1832, reveals that the President was prepared to be conciliatory as well as bellicose during the nullification crisis. The "Proclamation" is distinguished by its lucid analysis of the nature of the American Union and by Jackson's reasoned appeal to the "fellow-citizens" of his "native state" of South Carolina.

President's Proclamation*

PROCLAMATION BY ANDREW JACKSON, PRESIDENT OF THE UNITED STATES

Whereas a convention assembled in the State of South Carolina have passed an ordinance by which they declare "that the several acts and parts of acts of the Congress of

---

* Reprinted from *Executive Documents,* 22 Congress, 2 Session, 1832, Vol. I, Doc. No. 45, pp. 78-92.

the United States purporting to be laws for the imposing
of duties and imposts on the importation of foreign commodities, and now having actual operation and effect within the United States, and more especially" two acts for the
same purposes passed on the 29th of May, 1828, and on
the 14th of July, 1832, "are unauthorized by the Constitution of the United States, and violate the true meaning and
intent thereof, and are null and void and no law," nor binding on the citizens of that State or its officers; and by the
said ordinance it is further declared to be unlawful for any
of the constituted authorities of the State or of the United
States to enforce the payment of the duties imposed by the
said acts within the same State, and that it is the duty of
the Legislature to pass such laws as may be necessary to
give full effect to the said ordinance:

And whereas by the said ordinance, it is further ordained,
that in no case of law or equity decided in the courts of
said State, wherein shall be drawn in question the validity
of the said ordinance, or of the acts of the Legislature that
may be passed to give it effect, or of the said laws of the
United States, no appeal shall be allowed to the Supreme
Court of the United States, nor shall any copy of the record
be permitted or allowed for that purpose, and that any person attempting to take such appeal shall be punished as
for contempt of court:

And, finally, the said ordinance declares that the people
of South Carolina will maintain the said ordinance at every
hazard; and that they will consider the passage of any act
by Congress abolishing or closing the ports of the said State
or otherwise obstructing the free ingress or egress of vessels to and from the said ports, or any other act of the Federal Government to coerce the State, shut up her ports,

destroy or harass her commerce, or to enforce the said acts otherwise than through the civil tribunals of the country, as inconsistent with the longer continuance of South Carolina in the Union, and that the people of the said State will thenceforth hold themselves absolved from all further obligation to maintain or preserve their political connection with the people of the other States, and will forthwith proceed to organize a separate government and do all other acts and things which sovereign and independent states may of right do:

And whereas the said ordinance prescribes to the people of South Carolina a course of conduct in direct violation of their duty as citizens of the United States, contrary to the laws of their country, subversive of its Constitution, and having for its object the destruction of the Union—that Union which, coeval with our political existence, led our fathers, without any other ties to unite them than those of patriotism and a common cause, through a sanguinary struggle to a glorious independence—that sacred Union, hitherto inviolate, which, perfected by our happy Constitution, has brought us, by the favor of Heaven, to a state of prosperity at home, and high consideration abroad, rarely, if ever, equaled in the history of nations. To preserve this bond of our political existence from destruction, to maintain inviolate this state of national honor and prosperity, and to justify the confidence my fellow-citizens have reposed in me, I, Andrew Jackson, President of the United States, have thought proper to issue this my proclamation, stating my views of the Constitution and laws applicable to the measures adopted by the convention of South Carolina, and to the reasons they have put forth to sustain them, declaring the course which duty will require me to pursue, and, appealing to the understanding and patriotism of the people, warn them of the consequences that must inevitably result from an observance of the dictates of the convention.

Strict duty would require of me nothing more than the exercise of those powers with which I am now or may hereafter be invested for preserving the peace of the Union and for the execution of the laws. But the imposing aspect which opposition has assumed in this case, by clothing itself with State authority, and the deep interest which the people of the United States must all feel in preventing a resort to stronger measures while there is a hope that anything will be yielded to reasoning and remonstrance, perhaps demand, and will certainly justify, a full exposition to South Carolina and the nation of the views I entertain of this important question, as well as a distinct enunciation of the course which my sense of duty will require me to pursue.

The ordinance is founded, not on the indefeasible right of resisting acts which are plainly unconstitutional and too oppressive to be endured, but on the strange position that any one State may not only declare an act of Congress void, but prohibit its execution—that they may do this consistently with the Constitution—that the true construction of that instrument permits a State to retain its place in the Union, and yet be bound by no other of its laws than those it may choose to consider as constitutional. It is true, they add, that to justify this abrogation of a law it must be palpably contrary to the Constitution; but it is evident that to give the right of resisting laws of that description, coupled with the uncontrolled right to decide what laws deserve that character, is to give the power of resisting all laws.

For as, by the theory, there is no appeal, the reasons alleged by the State, good or bad, must prevail. If it should be said that public opinion is a sufficient check against the abuse of this power, it may be asked why it is not deemed a sufficient guard against the passage of an unconstitutional act of Congress? There is, however, a restraint in this last case, which makes the assumed power of a State more indefensible, and which does not exist in the other. There are two appeals from an unconstitutional act passed by Congress—one to the judiciary, the other to the people and the States. There is no appeal from the State decision in theory, and the practical illustration shows that the courts are closed against an application to review it, both judges and jurors being sworn to decide in its favor. But reasoning on this subject is superfluous, when our social compact, in express terms, declares that the laws of the United States, its Constitution, and treaties made under it are the supreme law of the land; and, for greater caution, adds "that the judges in every State shall be bound thereby, anything in the constitution or laws of any State to the contrary notwithstanding." And it may be asserted without fear of refutation that no Federative Government could exist without a similar provision. Look for a moment to the consequence. If South Carolina considers the revenue laws unconstitutional and has a right to prevent their execution in the port of Charleston, there would be a clear constitutional objection to their collection in every other port, and no revenue could be collected anywhere; for all imposts must be equal. It is no answer to repeat that an unconstitutional law is no law so long as the question of its legality is to be decided by the State itself; for every law operating injuriously upon any local interest will be perhaps thought, and certainly represented, as unconstitutional, and, as has been shown, there is no appeal.

If this doctrine had been established at an earlier day, the Union would have been dissolved in its infancy. The excise law in Pennsylvania, the embargo and non-intercourse law in the Eastern States, the carriage tax in Virginia, were all deemed unconstitutional, and were more unequal in their operation than any of the laws now complained of; but, fortunately, none of those States discovered that they had the right now claimed by South Carolina. The war, into which we were forced to support the dignity of the nation and the rights of our citizens, might have ended in defeat and disgrace, instead of victory and honor, if the States who supposed it a ruinous and unconstitutional measure had thought they possessed the right of nullifying the act by which it was declared and denying supplies for its prosecution. Hardly and unequally as those measures bore upon several members of the Union, to the legislatures of none did this efficient and peaceable remedy, as it is called, suggest itself. The discovery of this important feature in our Constitution was reserved to the present day. To the statesmen of South Carolina belongs the invention, and upon the citizens of that State will unfortunately fall the evils of reducing it to practice.

If the doctrine of a State veto upon the laws of the Union carries with it internal evidence of its impracticable absurdity, our constitutional history will also afford abundant proof that it would have been repudiated with indignation had it been proposed to form a feature in our Government.

In our colonial state, although dependent on another power, we very early considered ourselves as connected by common interest with each other. Leagues were formed for common defense, and before the declaration of independence we were known in our aggregate character as *the United Colonies of America.* That decisive and important step was taken jointly. We declared ourselves a nation by a joint, not by several acts, and when the terms of our Confederation were reduced to form it was in that of a solemn league of several States, by which they agreed that they would collectively form one nation for the purpose of conducting some certain domestic concerns and all foreign relations. In the instrument forming that Union is found an article which declares that "every State shall abide by the determinations of Congress on all questions which by that Confederation should be submitted to them."

Under the Confederation, then, no State could legally annul a decision of the Congress or refuse to submit to its execution; but no provision was made to enforce these decisions. Congress made requisitions, but they were not complied with. The Government could not operate on individuals. They had no judiciary, no means of collecting revenue.

But the defects of the Confederation need not be detailed. Under its operation we could scarcely be called a nation. We had neither prosperity at home nor consideration abroad. This state of things could not be endured, and our present happy Constitution was formed, but formed in vain if this fatal doctrine prevails. It was formed for important objects that are announced in the preamble, made in the name and by the authority of the people of the United States, whose delegates framed and whose conventions approved it. The most important among these objects—that which is placed first in rank, on which all the others rest—is *"to form a more perfect union."* Now, is it possible than even if there were no express provision giving supremacy to the Constitution and laws of the United States over those of the States, can it be conceived that an instrument made for the purpose of *"forming a more perfect union"* than that of the Confederation could be so constructed by the assembled wisdom of our country as to substitute for that Confederation a form of government dependent for its existence on the local interest, the party spirit, of a State, or of a prevailing faction in a State? Every man of plain, unsophisticated understanding who hears the question will give such an answer as will preserve the Union. Metaphysical subtlety, in pursuit of an impracticable theory, could alone have devised one that is calculated to destroy it.

I consider, then, the power to annul a law of the United States, assumed by one State, *incompatible with the existence of the Union, contradicted expressly by the letter of the Constitution, unauthorized by its spirit, inconsistent with every principle on which it was founded, and destructive of the great object for which it was formed.*

After this general view of the leading principle, we must examine the particular application of it which is made in the ordinance.

The preamble rests its justification on these grounds: It assumes, as a fact, that the obnoxious laws, although they purport to be laws for raising revenue, were in reality intended for the protection of manufactures, which purpose it asserts to be unconstitutional; that the operation of these laws is unequal; that the amount raised by them is greater than is required by the wants of the Government; and, finally, that the proceeds are to be applied to objects unauthorized by the Constitution. These are the only causes alleged to justify an open opposition to the laws of the country, and a threat of seceding from the Union, if any attempt should be made to enforce them. The first virtually acknowledges that the law in question was passed under a power expressly given by the Constitution to lay and collect imposts; but its constitutionality is drawn in question from the *motives* of those who passed it. However apparent this purpose may be in the present case, nothing can be more dangerous than to admit the position that an unconstitutional purpose entertained by the members who assent to a law enacted under a constitutional power shall make that law void: for how is that purpose to be ascertained? Who is to make the scrutiny? How often may bad purposes be falsely imputed—in how many cases are they concealed by false professions—in how many is no declaration of motive made? Admit this doctrine, and you give to the States an uncontrolled right to decide, and every law may be annulled under this pretext. If, therefore, the absurd and dangerous doctrine should be admitted, that a State may annul an unconstitutional law, or one that it deems such, it will not apply to the present case.

The next objection is, that the laws in question operate unequally. This objection may be made with truth to every law that has been or can be passed. The wisdom of man never yet contrived a system of taxation that would operate with perfect equality. If the unequal operation of a law makes it unconstitutional, and if all laws of that description may be abrogated by any State for that cause, then, indeed, is the Federal Constitution unworthy of the slightest effort for its preservation. We have hitherto relied on it as the perpetual bond of our Union. We have received it as the work of the assembled wisdom of the

nation. We have trusted to it as to the sheet anchor of
our safety in the stormy times of conflict with a foreign or
domestic foe. We have looked to it with sacred awe as the
palladium of our liberties, and with all the solemnities of
religion have pledged to each other our lives and fortunes
here and our hopes of happiness hereafter in its defense
and support. Were we mistaken, my countrymen, in at-
taching this importance to the Constitution of our country?
Was our devotion paid to the wretched, inefficient, clumsy
contrivance which this new doctrine would make it? Did
we pledge ourselves to the support of an airy nothing—a
bubble that must be blown away by the first breath of
disaffection? Was this self-destroying, visionary theory the
work of the profound statesmen, the exalted patriots, to
whom the task of constitutional reform was intrusted? Did
the name of Washington sanction, did the States deliberately ratify, such an anomaly in the history of fundamental
legislation? No. We were not mistaken. The letter of this
great instrument is free from this radical fault. Its language directly contradicts the imputation: its spirit—its
evident intent, contradicts it. No, we did not err! Our
Constitution does not contain the absurdity of giving power
to make laws, and another to resist them. The sages, whose
memory will always be reverenced, have given us a practical and, as they hoped, a permanent constitutional compact. The Father of his Country did not affix his revered
name to so palpable an absurdity. Nor did the States,
when they severally ratified it, do so under the impression
that a veto on the laws of the United States was reserved
to them or that they could exercise it by implication. Search
the debates in all their conventions, examine the speeches
of the most zealous opposers of federal authority, look at

the amendments that were proposed—they are all silent—not a syllable uttered, not a vote given, not a motion made to correct the explicit supremacy given to the laws of the Union over those of the States, or to show that implication, as is now contended, could defeat it. No, we have not erred! The Constitution is still the object of our reverence, the bond of our Union, our defense in danger, the source of our prosperity in peace: it shall descend, as we have received it, uncorrupted by sophistical construction, to our posterity, and the sacrifices of local interest, of State prejudices, of personal animosities, that were made to bring it into existence, will again be patriotically offered for its support.

The two remaining objections made by the ordinance to these laws, are, that the sums intended to be raised by them are greater than are required and that the proceeds will be unconstitutionally employed.

The Constitution has given, expressly, to Congress the right of raising revenue and of determining the sum the public exigencies will require. The States have no control over the exercise of this right, other than that which results from the power of changing the representatives who abuse it, and thus procure redress. Congress may undoubtedly abuse this discretionary power, but the same may be said of others with which they are vested. Yet the discretion must exist somewhere. The Constitution has given it to the representatives of all the people, checked by the representatives of the States and by the Executive power. The South Carolina construction gives it to the Legislature or the convention of a single State, where neither the people of the different States, nor the States in their separate capacity, nor the Chief Magistrate elected by the people have any representation. Which is the most discreet disposition of the power? I do not ask you, fellow-citizens, which is the constitutional disposition; that instrument speaks a language not to be misunderstood. But if you were assembled in general convention, which would you think the safest depository of this discretionary power in the last resort? Would you add a clause giving it to each of the States, or would you sanction the wise provisions already made by your Constitution? If this should be the result of your deliberations when providing for the future, are you, can you, be ready to risk all that we hold dear, to establish, for a temporary and a local purpose, that which you must acknowledge to be destructive, and even absurd, as a general provision? Carry out the consequences of this right vested in the different States, and you must perceive that the crisis your conduct presents at this day would recur whenever any law of the United States displeased any of the States, and that we should soon cease to be a nation.

The ordinance, with the same knowledge of the future that characterizes a former objection, tells you that the proceeds of the tax will be unconstitutionally applied. If this could be ascertained with certainty, the objection would with more propriety be reserved for the law so applying the proceeds, but surely can not be urged against the laws levying the duty.

These are the allegations contained in the ordinance. Examine them seriously, my fellow-citizens; judge for yourselves. I appeal to you to determine whether they are so clear, so convincing, as to leave no doubt of their correctness: and even if you should come to this conclusion, how far they justify the reckless, destructive course which you are directed to pursue. Review these objections and the conclusions drawn from them once more. What are they? Every law, then, for raising revenue, according to the South Carolina ordinance, may be rightfully annulled, unless it be so framed as no law ever will or can be framed. Congress have a right to pass laws for raising revenue, and each State have a right to oppose their execution—two rights directly opposed to each other; and yet is this absurdity supposed to be contained in an instrument drawn for the express purpose of avoiding collisions between the States and the General Government by an assembly of the most enlightened statesmen and purest patriots ever embodied for a similar purpose.

In vain have these sages declared that Congress shall have power to lay and collect taxes, duties, imposts, and excises; in vain have they provided that they shall have power to pass laws which shall be necessary and proper to carry those powers into execution, that those laws and that Constitution shall be the "supreme law of the land, and that the judges in every State shall be bound thereby, anything in the constitution or laws of any State to the contrary notwithstanding"; in vain have the people of the several States solemnly sanctioned these provisions, made them their paramount law, and individually sworn to support them whenever they were called on to execute any office. Vain provisions! ineffectual restrictions! vile profanation of oaths! miserable mockery of legislation! if a bare majority of the voters in any one State may, on a real or supposed knowledge of the intent with which a law has been passed, declare themselves free from its operation—say, here it gives too little; there, too much, and operates unequally—here it suffers articles to be free that ought to be taxed—there it taxes those that ought to be free—in this case the proceeds are intended to be applied to purposes which we do not approve—in that, the amount raised is more than is wanted.

Congress, it is true, are invested by the Constitution with the right of deciding these questions according to their sound discretion. Congress is composed of the representatives of all the States, and of all the people of all the States; but *we*, part of the people of one State, to whom the Constitution has given no power on the subject, from whom it has expressly taken it away—*we*, who have solemnly agreed that this Constitution shall be our law—*we*, most of whom have sworn to support it—*we* now abrogate this law and swear, and force others to swear, that it shall not be obeyed. And we do this not because Congress have no right to pass such laws—this we do not allege—but because they have passed them with improper views. They are unconstitutional from the motives of those who passed them, which we can never with certainty know; from their unequal operation, although it is impossible, from the nature of things, that they should be equal; and from the disposition which we presume may be made of their proceeds, although that disposition has not been declared. This is the plain meaning of the ordinance in relation to laws which it abrogates for alleged unconstitutionality. But it does not stop there. It repeals in express terms an important part of the Constitution itself and of laws passed to give it effect, which have never been alleged to be unconstitutional. The Constitution declares that the judicial powers of the United States extend to cases arising under the laws of the United States, and that such laws, the Constitution, and treaties shall be paramount to the State constitutions and laws. The judiciary act prescribes the mode by which the case may be brought before a court of the United States by appeal when a State tribunal shall decide against this provision of the Constitution. The ordinance declares there shall be no appeal; makes the State law paramount to the Constitution and laws of the United States; forces judges and jurors to swear that they will disregard their provisions; and even makes it penal in a suitor to attempt relief by appeal. It further declares that it shall not be lawful for the authorities of the United States or of that State to enforce the payment of duties imposed by the revenue laws within its limits.

Here is a law of the United States, not even pretended to be unconstitutional, repealed by the authority of a small majority of the voters of a single State. Here is a provision of the Constitution which is solemnly abrogated by the same authority.

On such expositions and reasonings the ordinance grounds not only an assertion of the right to annul the laws of which it complains, but to enforce it by a threat of seceding from the Union if any attempt is made to execute them.

This right to secede is deduced from the nature of the Constitution, which, they say, is a compact between sovereign States who have preserved their whole sovereignty and, therefore, are subject to no superior; that because they made the compact, they can break it when, in their opinion, it has been departed from by the other States. Fallacious as this course of reasoning is, it enlists State pride and finds advocates in the honest prejudices of those who have not studied the nature of our Government sufficiently to see the radical error on which it rests.

The people of the United States formed the Constitution, acting through the State legislatures in making the compact, to meet and discuss its provisions, and acting in separate conventions when they ratified those provisions; but the terms used in its construction show it to be a Government in which the people of all the States collectively are represented. We are *one people* in the choice of President and Vice President. Here the States have no other agency than to direct the mode in which the votes shall be given. The candidates having the majority of all the votes are chosen. The electors of a majority of States may have given their votes for one candidate, and yet another may be chosen. The people, then, and not the States, are represented in the Executive branch.

In the House of Representatives there is this difference, that the people of one State do not, as in the case of President and Vice President, all vote for the same officers. The people of all the States do not vote for all the members, each State electing only its own representatives. But this creates no material distinction. When chosen, they are all representatives of the United States, not representatives of the particular State from which they come. They are paid by the United States, not by the State, nor are they accountable to it for any act done in the performance of their legislative functions; and however they may in practice, as it is their duty to do, consult and prefer the interests of their particular constituents when they come in conflict with any other partial or local interest, yet it is their first and highest duty, as representatives of the United States, to promote the general good.

The Constitution of the United States, then, forms a *government,* not a league; and whether it be formed by compact between the States or in any other manner, its character is the same. It is a Government in which all the people are represented, which operates directly on the people individually, not upon the States—they retained all the power they did not grant. But each State, having expressly parted with so many powers as to constitute, jointly with the other States, a single nation, cannot, from that period, possess any right to secede, because such secession does not break a league, but destroys the unity of a nation; and any injury to that unity is not only a breach which would result from the contravention of a compact, but it is an offense against the whole Union. To say that any State may at pleasure secede from the Union is to say that the United States are not a nation; because it would be a solecism to contend that any part of a nation might dissolve its connection with the other parts, to their injury or ruin, without committing any offense. Secession, like any other revolutionary act, may be morally justified by the extremity of oppression; but to call it a constitutional right is confounding the meaning of terms; and can only be done through gross error or to deceive those who are willing to assert a right, but would pause before they made a revolution or incur the penalties consequent on a failure.

Because the Union was formed by a compact, it is said the parties to that compact may, when they feel themselves aggrieved, depart from it; but it is precisely because it is a compact that they cannot. A compact is an agreement or binding obligation. It may by its terms have a sanction or penalty for its breach, or it may not. If it contains no sanction, it may be broken with no other consequence than moral guilt; if it have a sanction, then the breach incurs the designated or implied penalty. A league between independent nations, generally, has no sanction other than a moral one; or if it should contain a penalty, as there is no common superior it cannot be enforced. A government, on the contrary, always has a sanction, express or implied; and in our case it is both necessarily implied and expressly given. An attempt, by force of arms, to destroy a government is an offense, by whatever means the constitutional compact may have been formed, and such government has the right by the law of self-defense to pass acts for punishing the offender, unless that right is modified, restrained, or resumed by the constitutional act. In our system, although it is modified in the case of treason, yet authority is expressly given to pass all laws necessary to carry its powers into effect, and under this grant provision has been made for punishing acts which obstruct the due administration of the laws.

It would seem superfluous to add anything to show the nature of that union which connects us; but, as erroneous opinions on this subject are the foundation of doctrines the most destructive to our peace, I must give some further development to my views on this subject. No one, fellow-citizens, has a higher reverence for the reserved rights of the States than the Magistrate who now addresses you. No one would make greater personal sacrifices or official exertions to defend them from violation; but equal care must be taken to prevent, on their part, an improper interference with or resumption of the rights they have vested in the nation. The line has not been so distinctly drawn as to avoid doubts in some cases of the exercise of power. Men of the best intentions and soundest views may differ in their construction of some parts of the Constitution; but there are others on which dispassionate reflection can leave no doubt. Of this nature appears to be the assumed right of secession. It rests, as we have seen, on the alleged undivided sovereignty of the States and on their having formed in this sovereign capacity a compact which is called the Constitution, from which, because they made it, they have the right to secede. Both of these positions are erroneous, and some of the arguments to prove them so have been anticipated.

The States severally have not retained their entire sovereignty. It has been shown that in becoming parts of a nation, not members of a league, they surrendered many of their essential parts of sovereignty. The right to make treaties—declare war—levy taxes—exercise exclusive judicial and legislative powers—were all of them functions of sovereign power. The States, then, for all these important purposes were no longer sovereign. The allegiance of their citizens was transferred, in the first instance, to the Government of the United States: they became American citizens and owed obedience to the Constitution of the United States and to laws made in conformity with the powers it vested in Congress. This last position has not been and cannot be denied. How then can that State be said to be sovereign and independent, whose citizens owe obedience to laws not made by it, and whose magistrates are sworn to disregard those laws when they come in conflict with those passed by another? What shows conclusively that the States cannot be said to have reserved an undivided sovereignty is that they expressly ceded the right to punish treason, not treason against their separate power, but treason against the United States. Treason is an offense against *sovereignty*, and sovereignty must reside with the power to punish it. But the reserved rights of the States are not less sacred because they have, for their common interest, made the General Government the depository of these powers.

The unity of our political character (as has been shown for another purpose) commenced with its very existence. Under the royal Government we had no separate character; our opposition to its oppressions began as *united colonies*. We were the *United States* under the Confederation, and the name was perpetuated and the Union rendered more perfect by the Federal Constitution. In none of these stages did we consider ourselves in any other light than as forming one nation. Treaties and alliances were made in the name of all. Troops were raised for the joint defense. How, then, with all these proofs that under all changes of our position we had, for designated purposes and with defined powers, created national governments, how is it that the most perfect of those several modes of union should now be considered as a mere league that may be dissolved at pleasure? It is from an abuse of terms. Compact is used as synonymous with league, although the true term is not employed, because it would at once show the fallacy of the reasoning. It would not do to say that our Constitution was only a league, but it is labored to prove it a compact (which in one sense it is) and then to argue that as a league is a compact every compact between nations must of course be a league, and that from such an engagement every sovereign power has a right to recede. But it has been shown that in this sense the States are not sovereign, and that even if they were, and the national Constitution had been formed by compact, there would be no right in any one State to exonerate itself from its obligations.

So obvious are the reasons which forbid this secession that it is necessary only to allude to them. The Union was formed for the benefit of all. It was produced by mutual sacrifices of interests and opinions. Can those sacrifices be recalled? Can the States who magnanimously surrendered their title to the territories of the West recall the grant? Will the inhabitants of the inland States agree to pay the duties that may be imposed without their assent by those on the Atlantic or the Gulf for their own benefit? Shall there be a free port in one State and onerous duties in another? No one believes that any right exists in a single State to involve all the others in these and countless other evils contrary to engagements solemnly made. Everyone must see that the other States, in self-defense, must oppose it at all hazards.

These are the alternatives that are presented by the convention: a repeal of all the acts for raising revenue, leaving the Government without the means of support, or an acquiescence in the dissolution of our Union by the secession of one of its members. When the first was proposed, it was known that it could not be listened to for a moment. It was known, if force was applied to oppose the execution of the laws, that it must be repelled by force; that Congress could not, without involving itself in disgrace and the country in ruin, accede to the proposition; and yet, if this is not done in a given day, or if any attempt is made to execute the laws, the State is by the ordinance declared to be out of the Union. The majority of a convention assembled for the purpose have dictated these terms, or rather this rejection of all terms, in the name of the people of South Carolina. It is true that the Governor of the State speaks of the submission of their grievances to a convention of all the States, which, he says, they "sincerely and anxiously seek and desire." Yet this obvious and constitutional mode of obtaining the sense of the other States on the construction of the federal compact, and amending it, if necessary, has never been attempted by those who have urged the State on to this destructive measure. The State might have proposed the call for a general convention to the other States, and Congress, if a sufficient number of them concurred, must have called it. But the first magistrate of South Carolina, when he expressed a hope that "on a review by Congress and the functionaries of the General Government of the merits of the controversy," such a convention will be accorded to them, must have known that neither Congress nor any functionary of the General Government has authority to call such a convention unless it be demanded by two-thirds of the States. This suggestion, then, is another instance of the reckless inattention to the provisions of the Constitution with which this crisis has been madly hurried on; or of the attempt to persuade the people that a constitutional remedy had been sought and refused. If the Legislature of South Carolina "anxiously desire" a general convention to consider their complaints, why have they not made application for it in the way the Constitution points out? The assertion that they "earnestly seek it," is completely negatived by the omission.

This, then, is the position in which we stand. A small majority of the citizens of one State in the Union have elected delegates to a State convention; that convention has ordained that all the revenue laws of the United States must be repealed, or that they are no longer a member of the Union. The Governor of that State has recommended to the Legislature the raising of an army to carry the secession into effect, and that he may be empowered to give clearances to vessels in the name of the State. No act of violent opposition to the laws has yet been committed, but such a state of things is hourly apprehended; and it is the intent of this instrument to *proclaim,* not only that the duty imposed on me by the Constitution "to take care that the laws be faithfully executed" shall be performed to the extent of the powers already vested in me by law, or of such others as the wisdom of Congress shall devise and intrust to me for that purpose, but to warn the citizens of South Carolina who have been deluded into an opposition to the laws of the danger they will incur by obedience to the illegal and disorganizing ordinance of the convention; to exhort those who have refused to support it to persevere in their determination to uphold the Constitution and laws of their country; and to point out to all the perilous situation into which the good people of that State have been led, and that the course they are urged to pursue is one of ruin and disgrace to the very State whose rights they affect to support.

Fellow-citizens of my native State, let me not only admonish you, as the First Magistrate of our common country, not to incur the penalty of its laws, but use the influence that a father would over his children whom he saw rushing to certain ruin. In that paternal language, with that paternal feeling, let me tell you, my countrymen, that you are deluded by men who are either deceived themselves or wish to deceive you. Mark under what pretenses you have been led on to the brink of insurrection and treason on which you stand! First, a diminution of the value of your staple commodity, lowered by overproduction in other quarters, and the consequent diminution in the value of your lands were the sole effect of the tariff laws.

The effect of those laws was confessedly injurious, but the evil was greatly exaggerated by the unfounded theory you were taught to believe, that its burthens were in proportion to your exports, not to your consumption of imported articles. Your pride was roused by the assertion that a submission to those laws was a state of vassalage and that resistance to them was equal in patriotic merit to the opposition our fathers offered to the oppressive laws of Great Britain. You were told that this opposition might be peaceably, might be constitutionally, made; that you might enjoy all the advantages of the Union and bear none of its burthens. Eloquent appeals to your passions, to your State pride, to your native courage, to your sense of real injury, were used to prepare you for the period when the mask which concealed the hideous features of *disunion* should be taken off. It fell, and you were made to look with complacency on objects which not long since you would have regarded with horror. Look back to the arts which have brought you to this state; look forward to the consequences to which it must inevitably lead! Look back to what was first told you as an inducement to enter into this dangerous course. The great political truth was repeated to you, that you had the revolutionary right of resisting all laws that were palpably unconstitutional and intolerably oppressive; it was added that the right to nullify a law rested on the same principle, but that it was a peaceable remedy! This character which was given to it made you receive with too much confidence the assertions that were made of the unconstitutionality of the law and its oppressive effects. Mark, my fellow-citizens, that by the admission of your leaders the unconstitutionality must be *palpable;* or it will not justify either resistance or nullification. What is the meaning of the word *palpable* in the sense in which it is here used? That which is apparent to everyone; that which no man of ordinary intellect will fail to perceive. Is the unconstitutionality of these laws of that description? Let those among your leaders who once approved and advocated the principle of protective duties answer the question; and let them choose whether they will be considered as incapable then of perceiving that which must have been apparent to every man of common understanding, or as imposing upon your confidence and endeavoring to mislead you now. In either case they are unsafe guides in the perilous path they urge you to tread. Ponder well on this circumstance, and you will know how to appreciate the exaggerated language they address to you. They are not champions of liberty, emulating the fame of our Revolutionary fathers; nor are you an oppressed people, contending, as they repeat to you, against worse than colonial vassalage.

You are free members of a flourishing and happy Union. There is no settled design to oppress you. You have indeed felt the unequal operation of laws which may have been unwisely, not unconstitutionally, passed; but that inequality must necessarily be removed. At the very moment when you were madly urged on to the unfortunate course you have begun a change in public opinion had commenced. The nearly approaching payment of the public debt and the consequent necessity of a diminution of duties had already produced a considerable reduction, and that, too, on some articles of general consumption in your State. The

importance of this change was underrated, and you were
authoritatively told that no further alleviation of your
burthens was to be expected at the very time when the
condition of the country imperiously demanded such a
modification of the duties as should reduce them to a just
and equitable scale. But, as if apprehensive of the effect
of this change in allaying your discontents, you were pre-
cipitated into the fearful state in which you now find yourselves.

I have urged you to look back to the means that were
used to hurry you on to the position you have now assumed
and forward to the consequences it will produce. Something more is necessary. Contemplate the condition of that
country of which you still form an important part. Consider its Government, uniting in one bond of common
interest and general protection so many different States,
giving to all their inhabitants the proud title of *American
citizen,* protecting their commerce, securing their litera-
ture and their arts, facilitating their intercommunication,
defending their frontiers, and making their name respected
in the remotest parts of the earth. Consider the extent of
its territory, its increasing and happy population, its advance in arts which render life agreeable, and the sciences
which elevate the mind! See education spreading the lights
of religion, morality, and general information into every
cottage in this wide extent of our Territories and States!
Behold it as the asylum where the wretched and the oppressed find a refuge and support! Look on this picture of
happiness and honor and say, *We too are citizens of America!* Carolina is one of these proud States; her arms have
defended, her best blood has cemented, this happy Union.
And then add, if you can, without horror and remorse, This

happy Union we will dissolve; this picture of peace and prosperity we will deface; this free intercourse we will interrupt; these fertile fields we will deluge with blood; the protection of that glorious flag we renounce; the very name of Americans we discard. And for what, mistaken men? For what do you throw away these inestimable blessings? For what would you exchange your share in the advantages and honor of the Union? For the dream of a separate independence—a dream interrupted by bloody conflicts with your neighbors and a vile dependence on a foreign power. If your leaders could succeed in establishing a separation, what would be your situation? Are you united at home? Are you free from the apprehension of civil discord, with all its fearful consequences? Do our neighboring republics, every day suffering some new revolution or contending with some new insurrection, do they excite your envy? But the dictates of a high duty oblige me solemnly to announce that you cannot succeed. The laws of the United States must be executed. I have no discretionary power on the subject; my duty is emphatically pronounced in the Constitution. Those who told you that you might peaceably prevent their execution deceived you; they could not have been deceived themselves. They know that a forcible opposition could alone prevent the execution of the laws, and they know that such opposition must be repelled. Their object is disunion. But be not deceived by names. Disunion by armed force is *treason*. Are you really ready to incur its guilt? If you are, on the heads of the instigators of the act be the dreadful consequences; on their heads be the dishonor, but on yours may fall the punishment. On your unhappy State will inevitably fall all the evils of the conflict you force upon the Government of your country. It cannot accede to the mad project of disunion, of which you would be the first victims. Its First Magistrate cannot, if he would, avoid the performance of his duty. The consequence must be fearful for you, distressing to your fellow-citizens here and to the friends of good government throughout the world. Its enemies have beheld our prosperity with a vexation they could not conceal; it was a standing refutation of their slavish doctrines, and they will point to our discord with the triumph of malignant joy. It is yet in your power to disappoint them. There is yet time to show that the descendants of the Pinckneys, the Sumpters, the Rutledges, and of the thousand other names which adorn the pages of your Revolutionary history will not abandon that Union to support which so many of them fought and bled and died.

I adjure you, as you honor their memory, as you love the cause of freedom, to which they dedicated their lives, as you prize the peace of your country, the lives of its best citizens, and your own fair fame, to retrace your steps. Snatch from the archives of your State the disorganizing edict of its convention; bid its members to reassemble and promulgate the decided expressions of your will to remain in the path which alone can conduct you to safety, prosperity, and honor. Tell them that compared to disunion all other evils are light, because that brings with it an accumulation of all. Declare that you will never take the field unless the star-spangled banner of your country shall float over you; that you will not be stigmatized when dead, and dishonored and scorned while you live, as the authors of the first attack on the Constitution of your country. Its destroyers you cannot be. You may disturb its peace, you may interrupt the course of its prosperity, you may cloud its reputation for stability; but its tranquillity will be restored, its prosperity will return, and the stain upon its national character will be transferred and remain an eternal blot on the memory of those who caused the disorder.

Fellow-citizens of the United States! The threat of unhallowed disunion, the names of those once respected by whom it is uttered, the array of military force to support it, denote the approach of a crisis in our affairs on which the continuance of our unexampled prosperity, our political existence, and perhaps that of all free governments may depend. The conjuncture demanded a free, a full, and explicit enunciation, not only of my intentions, but of my principles of action; and as the claim was asserted of a right by a State to annul the laws of the Union, and even to secede from it at pleasure, a frank exposition of my opinions in relation to the origin and form of our Government and the construction I give to the instrument by which it was created seemed to be proper. Having the fullest confidence in the justness of the legal and constitutional opinion of my duties which has been expressed, I rely with equal confidence on your undivided support in my determination to execute the laws, to preserve the Union by all constitutional means, to arrest, if possible, by moderate and firm measures the necessity of a recourse to force; and if it be the will of Heaven that the recurrence of its primeval curse on man for the shedding of a brother's blood should fall upon our land, that it be not called down by any offensive act on the part of the United States.

Fellow-citizens! The momentous case is before you. On your undivided support of your Government depends the decision of the great question it involves—whether your sacred Union will be preserved and the blessing it secures to us as one people shall be perpetuated. No one can doubt that the unanimity with which that decision will be expressed will be such as to inspire new confidence in republican institutions, and that the prudence, the wisdom, and the courage which it will bring to their defense will transmit them unimpaired and invigorated to our children.

May the Great Ruler of Nations grant that the signal blessings with which He has favored ours may not, by the madness of party or personal ambition, be disregarded and lost; and may His wise providence bring those who have produced this crisis to see the folly before they feel the misery of civil strife, and inspire a returning veneration for that Union which, if we may dare to penetrate His designs, He has chosen as the only means of attaining the high destinies to which we may reasonably aspire.

In testimony whereof I have caused the seal of the United States to be hereunto affixed, having signed the same with my hand.

Done at the city of Washington, this 10th day of December, A. D. 1832, and of the independence of the United States the fifty-seventh.

Andrew Jackson

By the President:
    EDW. LIVINGSTON,
        Secretary of State.

III. "NULLIFICATION IS DEAD"

THE NULLIFICATION struggle ended after Congress' adoption on March 1, 1833, of the Force Bill and the Compromise Tariff. Two months later Jackson summed up his estimate of both nullificationists and nullification in a letter to a Democratic office-holder.

To Rev. Andrew J. Crawford*

Private

Washington, May 1, 1833

. . . I have had a laborious task here, but nullification is dead; and its actors and exciters will only be remembered by the people to be execrated for their wicked designs to sever and destroy the only good government on the globe, and that prosperity and happiness we enjoy over every other portion of the world. Hamans gallows ought to be the fate of all such ambitious men who would involve their country in civil wars, and all the evils in its train, that they might reign and ride on its whirlwinds and direct the storm. The free people of these united States have spoken, and consigned these wicked demagogues to their proper doom. Take care of your nullifiers—you have them amongst you— let them meet with the indignant frowns of every man who loves his country. The tariff, it is *now* well known was a mere pretext—its burthen was on your course woollens. by the law of July 1832, course woollens was reduced to five per cent. for the benefit of the South. Mr. Clays bill takes it up and classes it with woollens, at 50 per cent. reduces it gradually down to 20 per cent. and there it is to remain and Mr. Calhoun and all the nullifiers agree to the prin-ciple. The cash duties and home valuation will be equal

---

* Reprinted from Bassett, *Correspondence of Andrew Jackson,* Vol. V, pp. 71-72. Reprinted with the permission of the Carnegie Institution of Washington. A facsimile of this letter is in the Massachusetts Historical Society.

to 15 per cent more, and after the year 1842 you pay on coarse woollens 35 percent, if this is not protection, I cannot understand—therefore the tariff was only the pretext and disunion and a southern confederacy the real object. The next pretext will be the negro, or slavery question. . . .

V • The Limits of Federal Authority

I. "An Honest Observance of Constitutional Compacts"

Although Jackson was a nationalist who believed in the supremacy of the Union over the states, he repeatedly emphasized both the rights and obligations of the states. He was aware that certain powers were reserved to the states, and he did not think that the Federal government should play a positive role in the nation's economy. Despite the aggressive leadership that he provided the American people, he favored a weak rather than a strong government and an economy in which there was a minimum of Federal interference. In his veto of the Maysville Road Bill he not only ignored the wishes of many of his Western supporters who advocated Federal aid for internal improvements, but he also spelled out his views on the limitations that the Constitution imposed on the authority of the central government.

To the House of Representatives*

Gentlemen: I have maturely considered the bill proposing to authorize "a subscription of stock in the Maysville, Washington, Paris, and Lexington Turnpike Road Com-

---

* Reprinted from *Journal of the House of Representatives of the United States*, 21 Congress, 1 Session, 1829-1830, pp. 733-742.

pany," and now return the same to the House of Representatives, in which it originated, with my objections to its passage.

Sincerely friendly to the improvement of our country by means of roads and canals, I regret that any difference of opinion in the mode of contributing to it should exist between us; and if in stating this difference I go beyond what the occasion may be deemed to call for, I hope to find an apology in the great importance of the subject, an unfeigned respect for the high source from which this branch of it has emanated, and an anxious wish to be correctly understood by my constituents in the discharge of all my duties. Diversity of sentiment among public functionaries actuated by the same general motives, on the character and tendency of particular measures, is an incident common to all governments, and the more to be expected in one which, like ours, owes its existence to the freedom of opinion, and must be upheld by the same influence. Controlled, as we thus are, by a higher tribunal, before which our respective acts will be canvassed with the indulgence due to the imperfections of our nature, and with that intelligence and unbiased judgment which are the true correctives of error, all that our responsibility demands is that the public good should be the measure of our views, dictating alike their frank expression and honest maintenance.

In the message which was presented to Congress at the opening of its present session, I endeavored to exhibit briefly my views upon the important and highly interesting subject to which our attention is now to be directed. I was desirous of presenting to the representatives of the several States in Congress assembled the inquiry whether some mode could not be devised which would reconcile the diversity of opinion concerning the powers of this Government over the subject of internal improvement, and the manner in which these powers, if conferred by the Constitution, ought to be exercised. The act which I am called upon to consider has, therefore, been passed with a knowledge of my views on this question, as these are expressed in the message referred to. In that document the following suggestions will be found:

After the extinction of the public debt it is not probable that any adjustment of the tariff upon principles satisfactory to the people of the Union will until a remote period, if ever, leave the Government without a considerable surplus in the Treasury beyond what may be required for its current service. As, then, the period approaches when the application of the revenue to the payment of debt will cease, the disposition of the surplus will present a subject for the serious deliberation of Congress; and it may be fortunate for the country that it is yet to be decided. Considered in connection with the difficulties which have heretofore attended appropriations for purposes of internal improvement, and with those which this experience tells us will certainly arise whenever power over such subjects may be exercised by the General Government, it is hoped that it may lead to the adoption of some plan which will reconcile the diversified interests of the States and strengthen the bonds which unite them. Every member of the Union, in peace and in war, will be benefited by the improvement of inland navigation and the construction of highways in the several States. Let us, then, endeavor to attain this benefit in a mode which will be satisfactory to all. That hitherto adopted has by many of our fellow-citizens been deprecated as an infraction of the Constitution, while by others it has been viewed as inexpedient. All feel that it has been employed at the expense of harmony in the legislative councils.

And adverting to the constitutional power of Congress to make what I considered a proper disposition of the surplus revenue, I subjoined the following remarks:

To avoid these evils it appears to me that the most safe, just, and federal disposition which could be made of the surplus revenue would be its apportionment among the several States according to their ratio of representation, and should this measure not be found warranted by the Constitution that it would be expedient to propose to the States an amendment authorizing it.

The constitutional power of the Federal Government to construct or promote works of internal improvement presents itself in two points of view—the first as bearing upon the sovereignty of the States within whose limits their execution is contemplated, if jurisdiction of the territory which they may occupy be claimed as necessary to their preservation and use; the second as asserting the simple right to appropriate money from the National Treasury in aid of such works when undertaken by State authority, surrendering the claim of jurisdiction. In the first view the question of power is an open one, and can be decided without the embarrassments attending the other, arising from the practice of the Government. Although frequently and strenuously attempted, the power to this extent has never been exercised by the Government in a single instance. It does not, in my opinion, possess it; and no bill, therefore, which admits it can receive my official sanction.

But in the other view of the power the question is differently situated. The ground taken at an early period of the Government was "that whenever money has been raised by the general authority and is to be applied to a particular measure, a question arises whether the particular measure be within the enumerated authorities vested in Congress. If it be, the money requisite for it may be applied to it; if not, no such application can be made." The document in which this principle was first advanced is of deservedly high authority, and should be held in grateful remembrance for its immediate agency in rescuing the country from much existing abuse and for its conservative effect upon some of the most valuable principles of the Constitution. The symmetry and purity of the Government would doubtless have been better preserved, if this restriction of the power of appropriation could have been maintained without weakening its ability to fulfill the general objects of its institution, an effect so likely to attend its admission, notwithstanding its apparent fitness, that every subsequent administration of the Government, embracing a period of thirty out of the forty-two years of its existence, has adopted a more enlarged construction of the power. It is not my purpose to detain you by a minute recital of the acts which sustain this assertion, but it is proper that I should notice some of the most prominent in order that the reflections which they suggest to my mind may be better understood.

In the administration of Mr. Jefferson we have two examples of the exercise of the right of appropriation, which in the considerations that led to their adoption and in their effects upon the public mind have had a greater agency in marking the character of the power than any subsequent events. I allude to the payment of $15,000,000 for the purchase of Louisiana and to the original appropriation for the construction of the Cumberland Road; the latter act deriving much weight from the acquiescence and approbation

of three of the most powerful of the original members of
the Confederacy, expressed through their respective legislatures. Although the circumstances of the latter case may
be such as to deprive so much of it as relates to the actual
construction of the road of the force of an obligatory exposition of the Constitution, it must, nevertheless, be admitted that so far as the mere appropriation of money is
concerned they present the principle in its most imposing
aspect. No less than twenty-three different laws have been
passed, through all the forms of the Constitution, appropriating upward of $2,500,000 out of the National Treasury
in support of that improvement, with the approbation of
every President of the United States, including my prede-
cessor, since its commencement.

Independently of the sanction given to appropriations
for the Cumberland and other roads and objects under this
power, the administration of Mr. Madison was character-
ized by an act which furnishes the strongest evidence of his
opinion of its extent. A bill was passed through both Houses
of Congress and presented for his approval, "setting apart
and pledging certain funds for constructing roads and canals and improving the navigation of water courses, in
order to facilitate, promote, and give security to internal
commerce among the several States and to render more
easy and less expensive the means and provisions for the
common defense." Regarding the bill as asserting a power
in the Federal Government to construct roads and canals
within the limits of the States in which they were made, he
objected to its passage on the ground of its unconstitutionality, declaring that the assent of the respective States in
the mode provided by the bill could not confer the power
in question; that the only cases in which the consent and

cession of particular States can extend the power of Congress are those specified and provided for in the Constitution, and superadding to these avowals his opinion that "a restriction of the power 'to provide for the common defense and general welfare' to cases which are to be provided for by the expenditure of money would still leave within the legislative power of Congress all the great and most important measures of Government, money being the ordinary and necessary means of carrying them into execution." I have not been able to consider these declarations in any other point of view than as a concession that the right of appropriation is not limited by the power to carry into effect the measure for which the money is asked, as was formerly contended.

The views of Mr. Monroe upon this subject were not left to inference. During his administration a bill was passed through both Houses of Congress, conferring the jurisdiction and prescribing the mode by which the Federal Government should exercise it in the case of the Cumberland Road. He returned it with objections to its passage, and in assigning them took occasion to say that in the early stages of the Government he had inclined to the construction that it had no right to expend money except in the performance of acts authorized by the other specific grants of power, according to a strict construction of them; but that on further reflection and observation his mind had undergone a change; that his opinion then was "that Congress have an unlimited power to raise money, and that in its appropriation they have a discretionary power, restricted only by the duty to appropriate it to purposes of common defense, and of general, not local, national, not State, benefit"; and this was avowed to be the governing principle through the residue of his administration. The views of the last administration are of such recent date as to render a particular reference to them unnecessary. It is well known that the appropriating power, to the utmost extent which had been claimed for it, in relation to internal improvements was fully recognized and exercised by it.

This brief reference to known facts will be sufficient to show the difficulty, if not impracticability, of bringing back the operations of the Government to the construction of the Constitution set up in 1798, assuming that to be its true reading in relation to the power under consideration: thus giving an admonitory proof of the force of implication and the necessity of guarding the Constitution with sleepless vigilance against the authority of precedents which have not the sanction of its most plainly defined powers. For, although it is the duty of all to look to that sacred instrument instead of the statute book, to repudiate at all times encroachments upon its spirit, which are too apt to be effected by the conjuncture of peculiar and facilitating circumstances, it is not less true that the public good and the nature of our political institutions require that individual differences should yield to a well-settled acquiescence of the people and confederated authorities in particular constructions of the Constitution on doubtful points. Not to concede this much to the spirit of our institutions would impair their stability and defeat the objects of the Constitution itself.

The bill before me does not call for a more definite opinion upon the particular circumstances which will warrant appropriations of money by Congress to aid works of internal improvement, for although the extension of the power to apply money beyond that of carrying into effect the object for which it is appropriated has, as we have seen, been long claimed and exercised by the Federal Government, yet such grants have always been professedly under the control of the general principle that the works which might be thus aided should be "of a general, not local—national, not State," character. A disregard of this distinction would of necessity lead to the subversion of the federal system. That even this is an unsafe one, arbitrary in its nature, and liable, consequently, to great abuses, is too obvious to require the confirmation of experience. It is, however, sufficiently definite and imperative to my mind to forbid my approbation of any bill having the character of the one under consideration. I have given to its provisions all the reflection demanded by a just regard for the interests of those of our fellow-citizens who have desired its passage, and by the respect which is due to a coordinate branch of the Government; but I am not able to view it in any other light than as a measure of purely local character; or, if it can be considered national, that no further distinction between the appropriate duties of the General and State Governments need be attempted; for there can be no local interest that may not with equal propriety be denominated national. It has no connection with any established system of improvements; is exclusively within the limits of a State, starting at a point on the Ohio River and running out 60 miles to an interior town, and even as far as the State is interested conferring partial instead of general advantages.

Considering the magnitude and importance of the power, and the embarrassments to which, from the very nature of the thing, its exercise must necessarily be subjected, the real friends of internal improvement ought not to be willing to confide it to accident and chance. What is properly *national* in its character or otherwise is an inquiry which is often extremely difficult of solution. The appropriations of one year for an object which is considered national may be rendered nugatory by the refusal of a succeeding Congress to continue the work on the ground that it is local. No aid can be derived from the intervention of corporations. The question regards the character of the work, not that of those by whom it is to be accomplished. Notwithstanding the union of the Government with the corporation by whose immediate agency any work of internal improvement is carried on, the inquiry will still remain—is it national and conducive to the benefit of the whole, or local and operating only to the advantage of a portion of the Union?

But although I might not feel it to be my official duty to interpose the Executive veto to the passage of a bill appropriating money for the construction of such works as are authorized by the States and are national in their character, I do not wish to be understood as expressing an opinion that it is expedient at this time for the General Government to embark in a system of this kind; and anxious that my constituents should be possessed of my views on this as well as on all other subjects which they have committed to my discretion, I shall state them frankly and briefly. Besides many minor considerations, there are two prominent views of the subject which have made a deep impression upon my mind, which, I think, are well entitled to your serious attention, and will, I hope, be maturely weighed by the people.

From the official communication submitted to you it appears that, if no adverse and unforeseen contingency happens in our foreign relations and no unusual diversion be made of the funds set apart for the payment of the national debt, we may look with confidence to its entire extinguishment in the short period of four years. The extent to which this pleasing anticipation is dependent upon the policy which may be pursued in relation to measures of the character of the one now under consideration must be obvious to all, and equally so that the events of the present session are well calculated to awaken public solicitude upon the subject. By the statement from the Treasury Department and those from the clerks of the Senate and House of Representatives, herewith submitted, it appears that the bills which have passed into laws, and those which in all probability will pass before the adjournment of Congress, anticipate appropriations which, with the ordinary expenditures for the support of Government, will exceed considerably the amount in the Treasury for the year 1830. Thus, whilst we are diminishing the revenue by a reduction of the duties on tea, coffee, and cocoa the appropriations for internal improvement are increasing beyond the available means of the Treasury; and if to this calculation be added the amounts contained in bills which are pending before the two Houses, it may be safely affirmed that ten millions of dollars would not make up the excess over the Treasury receipts, unless the payment of the national debt be postponed and the means now pledged to that object applied to those enumerated in these bills. Without a well-regulated system of internal improvement, this exhausting mode of appropriation is not likely to be avoided, and the plain consequence must be either a continuance of the national debt or a resort to additional taxes.

Although many of the States, with a laudable zeal and under the influence of an enlightened policy, are successfully applying their separate efforts to works of this character, the desire to enlist the aid of the General Government in the construction of such as from their nature ought to devolve upon it, and to which the means of the individual States are inadequate, is both rational and patriotic, and, if that desire is not gratified now, it does not follow that it never will be. The general intelligence and public spirit of the American people furnish a sure guaranty that at the proper time this policy will be made to prevail under circumstances more auspicious to its successful prosecution than those which now exist. But great as this object undoubtedly is, it is not the only one which demands the fostering care of the Government. The preservation and success of the republican principle rest with us. To elevate its character and extend its influence rank among our most important duties; and the best means to accomplish this desirable end are those which will rivet the attachment of our citizens to the Government of their choice by the comparative lightness of their public burthens and by the attraction which the superior success of its operations will present to the admiration and respect of the world. Through the favor of an overruling and indulgent Providence our country is blessed with general prosperity, and our citizens exempted from the pressure of taxation, which other less favored portions of the human family are obliged to bear; yet it is true that many of the taxes collected from our citizens through the medium of imposts have for a considerable period been onerous. In many particulars, these taxes have borne severely upon the laboring and less prosperous classes of the community, being imposed on the necessaries of life, and this, too, in cases where the burthen was not relieved by the consciousness that it would ultimately contribute to make us independent of foreign nations for articles of prime necessity by the encouragement of their growth and manufacture at home. They have been cheerfully borne because they were thought to be necessary to the support of Government and the payment of the debts unavoidably incurred in the acquisition and maintenance of our national rights and liberties. But have we a right to calculate on the same cheerful acquiescence, when it is known that the necessity for their continuance would cease were it not for irregular, improvident, and unequal appropriations of the public funds? Will not the people demand, as they have a right to do, such a prudent system of expenditure as will pay the debts of the Union and authorize the reduction of every tax to as low a point as the wise observance of the necessity to protect that portion of our manufactures and labor whose prosperity is essential to our national safety and independence will allow? When the national debt is paid, the duties upon those articles which we do not raise may be repealed with safety, and still leave, I trust, without oppression to any section of the country, an accumulating surplus fund, which may be beneficially applied to some well-digested system of improvement.

Under this view the question as to the manner in which the Federal Government can or ought to embark in the construction of roads and canals, and the extent to which it may impose burthens on the people for these purposes, may be presented on its own merits, free of all disguise and of every embarrassment, except such as may arise from the Constitution itself. Assuming these suggestions to be correct, will not our constituents require the observance of a course by which they can be effected? Ought they not to

require it? With the best disposition to aid, as far as I can
conscientiously, in furtherance of works of internal improvement, my opinion is that the soundest views of national policy at this time point to such a course. Besides
the avoidance of an evil influence upon the local concerns
of the country, how solid is the advantage which the Government will reap from it in the elevation of its character!
How gratifying the effect of presenting to the world the
sublime spectacle of a Republic of more than twelve millions of happy people, in the fifty-fourth year of her existence—after having passed through two protracted wars,
the one for the acquisition and the other for the maintenance of liberty—free from debt and with all her immense
resources unfettered! What a salutary influence would not
such an exhibition exercise upon the cause of liberal principles and free government throughout the world! Would
we not ourselves find in its effect an additional guaranty
that our political institutions will be transmitted to the
most remote posterity without decay? A course of policy
destined to witness events like these cannot be benefited
by a legislation which tolerates a scramble for appropriations that have no relation to any general system of improvement, and whose good effects must of necessity be
very limited. In the best view of these appropriations, the
abuses to which they lead far exceed the good which they
are capable of promoting. They may be resorted to as artful expedients to shift upon the Government the losses of
unsuccessful private speculation, and thus, by ministering
to personal ambition and self-aggrandizement, tend to sap
the foundations of public virtue and taint the administration of the Government with a demoralizing influence.

In the other view of the subject, and the only remaining one which it is my intention to present at this time, is involved the expediency of embarking in a system of internal improvement without a previous amendment of the Constitution explaining and defining the precise powers of the Federal Government over it. Assuming the right to appropriate money to aid in the construction of national works to be warranted by the cotemporaneous and continued exposition of the Constitution, its insufficiency for the successful prosecution of them must be admitted by all candid minds. If we look to usage to define the extent of the right, that will be found so variant and embracing so much that has been overruled as to involve the whole subject in great uncertainty and to render the execution of our respective duties in relation to it replete with difficulty and embarrassment. It is in regard to such works and the acquisition of additional territory that the practice obtained its first footing. In most, if not all, other disputed questions of appropriation the construction of the Constitution may be regarded as unsettled if the right to apply money in the enumerated cases is placed on the ground of usage.

This subject has been one of much, and, I may add, painful, reflection to me. It has bearings that are well calculated to exert a powerful influence upon our hitherto prosperous system of government, and which, on some accounts, may even excite despondency in the breast of an American citizen. I will not detain you with professions of zeal in the cause of internal improvements. If to be their friend is a virtue which deserves commendation, our country is blessed with an abundance of it; for I do not suppose there is an intelligent citizen who does not wish to see them flourish. But though all are their friends, but few, I trust, are unmindful of the means by which they should be promoted; none certainly are so degenerate as to desire their success at the cost of that sacred instrument with the preservation of which is indissolubly bound our country's hopes. If different impressions are entertained in any quarter; if it is expected that the people of this country, reckless of their constitutional obligations, will prefer their local interest to the principles of the Union, such expectations will in the end be disappointed; or if it be not so, then indeed has the world but little to hope from the example of free government. When an honest observance of constitutional compacts cannot be obtained from communities like ours, it need not be anticipated elsewhere, and the cause in which there has been so much martyrdom, and from which so much was expected by the friends of liberty, may be abandoned, and the degrading truth that man is unfit for self-government admitted. And this will be the case, if *expediency* be made a rule of construction in interpreting the Constitution. Power in no government could desire a better shield for the insidious advances which it is ever ready to make upon the checks that are designed to restrain its action.

But I do not entertain such gloomy apprehensions. If it be the wish of the people that the construction of roads and canals should be conducted by the Federal Government, it is not only highly expedient, but indispensably necessary, that a previous amendment of the Constitution, delegating the necessary power and defining and restricting its exercise with reference to the sovereignty of the States, should be made. Without it nothing extensively useful can be effected. The right to exercise as much jurisdiction as is necessary to preserve the works and to raise funds by the collection of tolls to keep them in repair cannot be dispensed with. The Cumberland Road should be an instructive admonition of the consequences of acting without this right. Year after year contests are witnessed, growing out of efforts to obtain the necessary appropriations for completing and repairing this useful work. Whilst one Congress may claim and exercise the power, a succeeding one may deny it; and this fluctuation of opinion must be unavoidably fatal to any scheme which from its extent would promote the interests and elevate the character of the country. The experience of the past has shown that the opinion of Congress is subject to such fluctuations.

If it be the desire of the people that the agency of the Federal Government should be confined to the appropriation of money in aid of such undertakings, in virtue of State authorities, then the occasion, the manner, and the extent of the appropriations should be made the subject of constitutional regulation. This is the more necessary in order that they may be equitable among the several States, promote harmony between different sections of the Union and their representatives, preserve other parts of the Constitution from being undermined by the exercise of doubtful powers or the too great extension of those which are not so, and protect the whole subject against the deleterious influence of combinations to carry by concert measures which, considered by themselves, might meet but little countenance.

That a constitutional adjustment of this power upon equitable principles is in the highest degree desirable can

scarcely be doubted; nor can it fail to be promoted by
every sincere friend to the success of our political institutions. In no government are appeals to the source of power
in cases of real doubt more suitable than in ours. No good
motive can be assigned for the exercise of power by the
constituted authorities, while those for whose benefit it is
to be exercised have not conferred it and may not be willing to confer it. It would seem to me that an honest application of the conceded powers of the General Government
to the advancement of the common weal present a sufficient scope to satisfy a reasonable ambition. The difficulty
and supposed impracticability of obtaining an amendment
of the Constitution in this respect is, I firmly believe, in a
great degree unfounded. The time has never yet been when
the patriotism and intelligence of the American people
were not fully equal to the greatest exigency; and it never
will when the subject calling forth their interposition is
plainly presented to them. To do so with the questions involved in this bill, and to urge them to an early, zealous,
and full consideration of their deep importance, is, in my
estimation, among the highest of our duties.

A supposed connection between appropriations for internal improvement and the system of protecting duties,
growing out of the anxieties of those more immediately
interested in their success, has given rise to suggestions
which it is proper I should notice on this occasion. My
opinions on these subjects have never been concealed from
those who had a right to know them. Those which I have
entertained on the latter have frequently placed me in opposition to individuals as well as communities whose claims
upon my friendship and gratitude are of the strongest char-

acter, but I trust there has been nothing in my public life which has exposed me to the suspicion of being thought capable of sacrificing my views of duty to private considerations, however strong they may have been or deep the regrets which they are capable of exciting.

As long as the encouragement of domestic manufactures is directed to national ends it shall receive from me a temperate but steady support. There is no necessary connection between it and the system of appropriations. On the contrary, it appears to me that the supposition of their dependence upon each other is calculated to excite the prejudices of the public against both. The former is sustained on the grounds of its consistency with the letter and spirit of the Constitution, of its origin being traced to the assent of all the parties to the original compact, and of its having the support and approbation of a majority of the people, on which account it is at least entitled to a fair experiment. The suggestions to which I have alluded refer to a forced continuance of the national debt by means of large appropriations as a substitute for the security which the system derives from the principles on which it has hitherto been sustained. Such a course would certainly indicate either an unreasonable distrust of the people or a consciousness that the system does not possess sufficient soundness for its support if left to their voluntary choice and its own merits. Those who suppose that any policy thus founded can be long upheld in this country have looked upon its history with eyes very different from mine. This policy, like every other, must abide the will of the people, who will not be likely to allow any device, however specious, to conceal its character and tendency.

In presenting these opinions I have spoken with the freedom and candor which I thought the occasion for their expression called for; and now respectfully return the bill which has been under consideration for your further deliberation and judgment.

Andrew Jackson

May 27, 1830

VI • Equality of Opportunity

I. "Equal Protection and Equal Benefits"

Jackson's message vetoing the bill to recharter the Second Bank of the United States contains the best single summary of his economic and governmental philosophies. In this statement he developed in detail his theory of economic individualism and his concept of the powers of the Federal government. Although he thought that in this instance the government had to intervene to prevent a corporation from destroying equality of economic opportunity, he warned the American people that their rights could be destroyed by a too-powerful government as well as by a privileged minority and that the government's "true strength" consisted "in leaving individuals and States as much as possible to themselves—in making itself felt, not in its power, but in its beneficence; not in its control, but in its protection."

To the Senate*

The bill "to modify and continue" the act entitled "An act to incorporate the subscribers to the Bank of the United States" was presented to me on the 4th July instant. Having considered it with that solemn regard to the principles

* Reprinted from *Journal of the Senate of the United States*, 22 Congress, 1 Session, 1831-1832, pp. 433-446.

of the Constitution which the day was calculated to inspire, and come to the conclusion that it ought not to become a law, I herewith return it to the Senate, in which it originated, with my objections.

A bank of the United States is in many respects convenient for the Government and useful to the people. Entertaining this opinion, and deeply impressed with the belief that some of the powers and privileges possessed by the existing bank are unauthorized by the Constitution, subversive of the rights of the States, and dangerous to the liberties of the people, I felt it my duty at an early period of my Administration to call the attention of Congress to the practicability of organizing an institution combining all its advantages and obviating these objections. I sincerely regret that in the act before me I can perceive none of those modifications of the bank charter which are necessary, in my opinion, to make it compatible with justice, with sound policy, or with the Constitution of our country.

The present corporate body, denominated the President, Directors, and Company of the Bank of the United States, will have existed, at the time this act is intended to take effect, twenty years. It enjoys an exclusive privilege of banking under the authority of the General Government, a monopoly of its favor and support, and, as a necessary consequence, almost a monopoly of the foreign and domestic exchange. The powers, privileges, and favors bestowed upon it in the original charter, by increasing the value of the stock far above its par value, operated as a gratuity of many millions to the stockholders.

An apology may be found for the failure to guard against this result in the consideration that the effect of the original act of incorporation could not be certainly foreseen at the time of its passage. The act before me proposes another gratuity to the holders of the same stock, and in many cases to the same men, of at least seven millions more. This donation finds no apology in any uncertainty as to the effect of the act. On all hands it is conceded that its passage will increase at least twenty or thirty per cent. more the market price of the stock, subject to the payment of the annuity of $200,000 per year secured by the act, thus adding in a moment one-fourth to its par value. It is not our own citizens only who are to receive the bounty of our Government. More than eight millions of the stock of this bank are held by foreigners. By this act the American Republic proposes virtually to make them a present of some millions of dollars. For these gratuities to foreigners and to some of our own opulent citizens, the act secures no equivalent whatever. They are the certain gains of the present stockholders under the operation of this act, after making full allowance for the payment of the bonus.

Every monopoly and all exclusive privileges are granted at the expense of the public, which ought to receive a fair equivalent. The many millions which this act proposes to bestow on the stockholders of the existing bank must come directly or indirectly out of the earnings of the American people. It is due to them, therefore, if their Government sell monopolies and exclusive privileges, that they should at least exact for them as much as they are worth in open market. The value of the monopoly in this case may be correctly ascertained. The twenty-eight millions of stock would probably be at an advance of fifty per cent., and command in market at least forty-two millions of dollars, subject to the payment of the present bonus. The present value of the monopoly, therefore, is seventeen millions of dollars, and this the act proposes to sell for three millions, payable in fifteen annual installments of $200,000 each.

It is not conceivable how the present stockholders can have any claim to the special favor of the Government. The present corporation has enjoyed its monopoly during the period stipulated in the original contract. If we must have such a corporation, why should not the Government sell out the whole stock and thus secure to the people the full market value of the privileges granted? Why should not Congress create and sell twenty-eight millions of stock, incorporating the purchasers with all the powers and privileges secured in this act and putting the premium upon the sales into the Treasury?

But this act does not permit competition in the purchase of this monopoly. It seems to be predicated on the erroneous idea that the present stockholders have a prescriptive right not only to the favor but to the bounty of Government. It appears that more than a fourth part of the stock is held by foreigners, and the residue is held by a few hundred of our own citizens, chiefly of the richest class. For their benefit does this act exclude the whole American people from competition in the purchase of this monopoly and dispose of it for many millions less than it is worth. This seems the less excusable because some of our citizens not now stockholders petitioned that the door of competition might be opened, and offered to take a charter on terms much more favorable to the Government and country.

But this proposition, although made by men whose aggregate wealth is believed to be equal to all the private stock in the existing bank, has been set aside, and the bounty of our Government is proposed to be again bestowed on the few who have been fortunate enough to secure the stock and at this moment wield the power of the existing institution. I cannot perceive the justice or policy of this course. If our Government must sell monopolies, it would seem to be its duty to take nothing less than their full value, and if gratuities must be made once in fifteen or twenty years let them not be bestowed on the subjects of a foreign government nor upon a designated and favored class of men in our own country. It is but justice and good policy, as far as the nature of the case will admit, to confine our favors to our own fellow citizens, and let each in his turn enjoy an opportunity to profit by our bounty. In the bearings of the act before me upon these points I find ample reasons why it should not become a law.

It has been urged as an argument in favor of rechartering the present bank that the calling in its loans will produce great embarrassment and distress. The time allowed to close its concerns is ample; and if it has been well managed its pressure will be light, and heavy only in case its management has been bad. If, therefore, it shall produce distress, the fault will be its own; and it would furnish a reason against renewing a power which has been so obviously abused. But will there ever be a time when this reason will be less powerful? To acknowledge its force is to admit that the bank ought to be perpetual, and as a consequence the present stockholders and those inheriting their rights as successors be established a privileged order, clothed both with great political power and enjoying immense pecuniary advantages from their connection with the Government.

The modifications of the existing charter proposed by

this act are not such, in my view, as make it consistent with
the rights of the States or the liberties of the people. The
qualification of the right of the bank to hold real estate, the
limitation of its power to establish branches, and the power
reserved to Congress to forbid the circulation of small notes
are restrictions comparatively of little value or importance.
All the objectionable principles of the existing corporation, and most of its odious features, are retained without
alleviation.

The fourth section provides "that the notes or bills of
the said corporation, although the same be, on the faces
thereof, respectively made payable at one place only, shall
nevertheless be received by the said corporation at the
bank or at any of the offices of discount and deposit thereof
if tendered in liquidation or payment of any balance or balances due to said corporation or to such office of discount
and deposit from any other incorporated bank." This provision secures to the State banks a legal privilege in the
Bank of the United States which is withheld from all private citizens. If a State bank in Philadelphia owe the Bank
of the United States and have notes issued by the St. Louis
branch, it can pay the debt with those notes; but if a merchant, mechanic, or other private citizen be in like circumstances he cannot by law pay his debt with those notes, but
must sell them at a discount or send them to St. Louis to
be cashed. This boon conceded to the State banks, though
not unjust in itself, is most odious because it does not measure out equal justice to the high and the low, the rich and
the poor. To the extent of its practical effect it is a bond
of union among the banking establishments of the nation,
erecting them into an interest separate from that of the
people, and its necessary tendency is to unite the Bank of

the United States and the State banks in any measure which may be thought conducive to their common interest.

The ninth section of the act recognizes principles of worse tendency than any provision of the present charter.

It enacts that "the cashier of the bank shall annually report to the Secretary of the Treasury the names of all stockholders who are not resident citizens of the United States, and on the application of the treasurer of any State shall make out and transmit to such treasurer a list of stockholders residing in or citizens of such State, with the amount of stock owned by each." Although this provision, taken in connection with a decision of the Supreme Court, surrenders, by its silence, the right of the States to tax the banking institutions created by this corporation under the name of branches throughout the Union, it is evidently intended to be construed as a concession of their right to tax that portion of the stock which may be held by their own citizens and residents. In this light, if the act becomes a law, it will be understood by the States, who will probably proceed to levy a tax equal to that paid upon the stock of banks incorporated by themselves. In some States that tax is now one per cent., either on the capital or on the shares, and that may be assumed as the amount which all citizen or resident stockholders would be taxed under the operation of this act. As it is only the stock *held* in the States and not that *employed* within them which would be subject to taxation, and as the names of foreign stockholders are not to be reported to the Treasurers of the States, it is obvious that the stock held by them will be exempt from this burden. Their annual profits will therefore be one per cent. more than the citizen stockholders, and as the annual dividends of the bank may be safely estimated at seven per cent., the stock will be worth ten or fifteen per cent. more to foreigners than to citizens of the United States. To appreciate the effects which this state of things will produce, we must take a brief review of the operations and present condition of the Bank of the United States.

By documents submitted to Congress at the present session it appears that on the 1st of January, 1832, of the twenty-eight millions of private stock in the corporation, $8,405,500 were held by foreigners, mostly of Great Britain. The amount of stock held in the nine Western and Southwestern States is $140,200, and in the four Southern States is $5,623,100, and in the Middle and Eastern States is about $13,522,000. The profits of the bank in 1831, as shown in a statement to Congress, were about $3,455,598; of this there accrued in the nine Western States about $1,640,048; in the four Southern States about $352,507, and in the Middle and Eastern States about $1,463,041. As little stock is held in the West, it is obvious that the debt of the people in that section to the bank is principally a debt to the Eastern and foreign stockholders; that the interest they pay upon it is carried into the Eastern States and into Europe, and that it is a burden upon their industry and a drain of their currency, which no country can bear without inconvenience and occasional distress. To meet this burden and equalize the exchange operations of the bank, the amount of specie drawn from those States through its branches within the last two years, as shown by its official reports, was about $6,000,000. More than half a million of this amount does not stop in the Eastern States, but passes on to Europe to pay the dividends of the foreign stockholders. In the principle of taxation recognized by this act the Western States find no adequate compensation for this perpetual burden on their industry and drain of their currency. The branch bank at Mobile made last year 95,140 dollars, yet under the provisions of this act the State of Alabama can raise no revenue from these profitable operations, because not a share of the stock is held by any of her citizens. Mississippi and Missouri are in the same condition in relation to the branches at Natchez and St. Louis, and such, in a greater or less degree, is the condition of every Western State. The tendency of the plan of taxation which this act proposes will be to place the whole United States in the same relation to foreign countries which the Western States now bear to the Eastern. When by a tax on resident stockholders the stock of this bank is made worth ten or fifteen per cent. more to foreigners than to residents, most of it will inevitably leave the country.

Thus will this provision in its practical effect deprive the Eastern as well as the Southern and Western States of the means of raising a revenue from the extension of business and great profits of this institution. It will make the American people debtors to aliens in nearly the whole amount due to this bank, and send across the Atlantic from two to five millions of specie every year to pay the bank dividends.

In another of its bearings this provision is fraught with danger. Of the twenty-five directors of this bank five are chosen by the Government and twenty by the citizen stockholders. From all voice in these elections the foreign stockholders are excluded by the charter. In proportion, therefore, as the stock is transferred to foreign holders the extent of suffrage in the choice of directors is curtailed. Already is almost a third of the stock in foreign hands and not represented in elections. It is constantly passing out

of the country, and this act will accelerate its departure.
The entire control of the institution would necessarily fall
into the hands of a few citizen stockholders, and the ease
with which the object would be accomplished would be a
temptation to designing men to secure that control in their
own hands by monopolizing the remaining stock. There
is danger that a president and directors would then be able
to elect themselves from year to year, and without responsibility or control manage the whole concerns of the bank
during the existence of its charter. It is easy to conceive
that great evils to our country and its institutions might
flow from such a concentration of power in the hands of a
few men irresponsible to the people.

Is there no danger to our liberty and independence in a
bank that in its nature has so little to bind it to our country? The president of the bank has told us that most of the
State banks exist by its forbearance. Should its influence
become concentered, as it may under the operation of such
an act as this, in the hands of a self-elected directory whose
interests are identified with those of the foreign stockholders, will there not be cause to tremble for the purity of our
elections in peace and for the independence of our country
in war? Their power would be great whenever they might
choose to exert it; but if this monopoly were regularly renewed every fifteen or twenty years on terms proposed by
themselves, they might seldom in peace put forth their
strength to influence elections or control the affairs of the
nation. But if any private citizen or public functionary
should interpose to curtail its powers or prevent a renewal
of its privileges, it cannot be doubted that he would be
made to feel its influence.

Should the stock of the bank principally pass into the

hands of the subjects of a foreign country, and we should unfortunately become involved in a war with that country, what would be our condition? Of the course which would be pursued by a bank almost wholly owned by the subjects of a foreign power, and managed by those whose interests, if not affections, would run in the same direction there can be no doubt. All its operations within would be in aid of the hostile fleets and armies without. Controlling our currency, receiving our public moneys, and holding thousands of our citizens in dependence, it would be more formidable and dangerous than the naval and military power of the enemy.

If we must have a bank with private stockholders, every consideration of sound policy and every impulse of American feeling admonishes that it should be *purely American.* Its stockholders should be composed exclusively of our own citizens, who at least ought to be friendly to our Government and willing to support it in times of difficulty and danger. So abundant is domestic capital that competition in subscribing for the stock of local banks has recently led almost to riots. To a bank exclusively of American stockholders, possessing the powers and privileges granted by this act, subscriptions for two hundred millions of dollars could be readily obtained. Instead of sending abroad the stock of the bank in which the Government must deposit its funds and on which it must rely to sustain its credit in times of emergency, it would rather seem to be expedient to prohibit its sale to aliens under penalty of absolute forfeiture.

It is maintained by the advocates of the bank that its constitutionality in all its features ought to be considered as settled by precedent and by the decision of the Supreme

Court. To this conclusion I cannot assent. Mere precedent is a dangerous source of authority, and should not be regarded as deciding questions of constitutional power except where the acquiescence of the people and the States can be considered as well settled. So far from this being the case on this subject, an argument against the bank might be based on precedent. One Congress, in 1791, decided in favor of a bank; another, in 1811, decided against it. One Congress, in 1815, decided against a bank; another, in 1816, decided in its favor. Prior to the present Congress, therefore, the precedents drawn from that source were equal. If we resort to the States, the expressions of legislative, judicial, and executive opinions against the bank have been probably to those in its favor as four to one. There is nothing in precedent, therefore, which, if its authority were admitted, ought to weigh in favor of the act before me.

If the opinion of the Supreme Court covered the whole ground of this act, it ought not to control the coordinate authorities of this Government. The Congress, the Executive, and the Court must each for itself be guided by its own opinion of the Constitution. Each public officer who takes an oath to support the Constitution swears that he will support it as he understands it, and not as it is understood by others. It is as much the duty of the House of Representatives, of the Senate, and of the President to decide upon the constitutionality of any bill or resolution which may be presented to them for passage or approval as it is of the Supreme Judges when it may be brought before them for judicial decision. The opinion of the judges has no more authority over Congress than the opinion of Congress has over the judges; and on that point the President is independent of both. The authority of the Supreme Court must not, therefore, be permitted to control the Congress or the Executive when acting in their legislative capacities, but to have only such influence as the force of their reasoning may deserve.

But in the case relied upon the Supreme Court have not decided that all the features of this corporation are compatible with the Constitution. It is true that the court have said that the law incorporating the bank is a constitutional exercise of power by Congress. But taking into view the whole opinion of the court and the reasoning by which they have come to that conclusion, I understand them to have decided that inasmuch as a bank is an appropriate means for carrying into effect the enumerated powers of the General Government, therefore the law incorporating it is in accordance with that provision of the Constitution which declares that Congress shall have power "to make all laws which shall be necessary and proper for carrying those powers into execution." Having satisfied themselves that the word "*necessary*" in the Constitution means "*needful,*" "*requisite,*" "*essential,*" "*conducive to,*" and that "a bank" is a convenient, a useful, and essential instrument in the prosecution of the Government's "fiscal operations," they conclude that to "use one must be within the discretion of Congress" and that "the act to incorporate the Bank of the United States is a law made in pursuance of the Constitution"; "but," say they, "*where the law is not prohibited and is really calculated to effect any of the objects intrusted to the Government, to undertake here to inquire into the degree of its necessity would be to pass the line which circumscribes the judicial department and to tread on legislative ground.*"

The principle here affirmed is that the "degree of its necessity," involving all the details of a banking institution, is a question exclusively for legislative consideration. A bank is constitutional, but it is the province of the Legislature to determine whether this or that particular power, privilege, or exemption is "necessary and proper" to enable the bank to discharge its duties to the Government, and from their decision there is no appeal to the courts of justice. Under the decision of the Supreme Court, therefore, it is the exclusive province of Congress and the President to decide whether the particular features of this act are *necessary* and *proper* in order to enable the bank to perform conveniently and efficiently the public duties assigned to it as a fiscal agent, and therefore constitutional, or *unnecessary* and *improper*, and therefore unconstitutional.

Without commenting on the general principle affirmed by the Supreme Court, let us examine the details of this act in accordance with the rule of legislative action which they have laid down. It will be found that many of the powers and privileges conferred on it cannot be supposed necessary for the purpose for which it is proposed to be created, and are not, therefore, means necessary to attain the end in view, and consequently not justified by the Constitution.

The original act of incorporation, section 21, enacts "that no other bank shall be established by any future law of the United States during the continuance of the corporation hereby created, for which the faith of the United States is hereby pledged: *Provided*, Congress may renew existing charters for banks within the District of Columbia not increasing the capital thereof, and may also establish any other bank or banks in said District with capitals not exceeding in the whole $6,000,000 if they shall deem it expedient." This provision is continued in force by the act before me fifteen years from the 3d of March, 1836.

If Congress possessed the power to establish one bank, they had power to establish more than one if in their opinion two or more banks had been "necessary" to facilitate the execution of the powers delegated to them in the Constitution. If they possessed the power to establish a second bank, it was a power derived from the Constitution to be exercised from time to time, and at any time when the interests of the country or the emergencies of the Government might make it expedient. It was possessed by one Congress as well as another, and by all Congresses alike, and alike at every session. But the Congress of 1816 have taken it away from their successors for twenty years, and the Congress of 1832 proposes to abolish it for fifteen years more. It cannot be *"necessary"* or *"proper"* for Congress to barter away or divest themselves of any of the powers vested in them by the Constitution to be exercised for the public good. It is not *"necessary"* to the efficiency of the bank, nor is it *"proper"* in relation to themselves and their successors. They may *properly* use the discretion vested in them, but they may not limit the discretion of their successors. This restriction on themselves and grant of a monopoly to the bank is, therefore, unconstitutional.

In another point of view this provision is a palpable attempt to amend the Constitution by an act of legislation. The Constitution declares that "the Congress shall have power to exercise exclusive legislation in all cases whatsoever" over the District of Columbia. Its constitutional power, therefore, to establish banks in the District of Columbia and increase their capital at will is unlimited and uncontrollable by any other power than that which gave authority to the Constitution. Yet this act declares that Congress shall *not* increase the capital of existing banks, nor create other banks with capitals exceeding in the whole six millions of dollars. The Constitution declares that Congress *shall* have power to exercise exclusive legislation over this District *"in all cases whatsoever,"* and this act declares they shall not. Which is the supreme law of the land? This provision cannot be *"necessary"* or *"proper"* or *constitutional* unless the absurdity be admitted that whenever it be "necessary and proper" in the opinion of Congress they have a right to barter away one portion of the powers vested in them by the Constitution as a means of executing the rest.

On two subjects only does the Constitution recognize in Congress the power to grant exclusive privileges or monopolies. It declares that "Congress shall have power to promote the progress of science and useful arts by securing for limited times to authors and inventors the exclusive right to their respective writings and discoveries." Out of this express delegation of power have grown our laws of patents and copyrights. As the Constitution expressly delegates to Congress the power to grant exclusive privileges in these cases as the means of executing the substantive power "to promote the progress of science and useful arts," it is consistent with the fair rules of construction to conclude that such a power was not intended to be granted as a means of accomplishing any other end. On every other subject which comes within the scope of Congressional power there is an ever-living discretion in the use of proper means, which cannot be restricted or abolished without an amendment of the Constitution. Every act of Congress, therefore, which attempts by grants of monopolies or sale of exclusive privileges for a limited time, or a time without limit, to restrict or extinguish its own discretion in the choice of means to execute its delegated powers is equivalent to a legislative amendment of the Constitution, and palpably unconstitutional.

This act authorizes and encourages transfers of its stock to foreigners and grants them an exemption from all State and national taxation. So far from being *"necessary and proper"* that the bank should possess this power to make it a safe and efficient agent of the Government in its fiscal operations, it is calculated to convert the Bank of the United States into a foreign bank, to impoverish our people in time of peace, to disseminate a foreign influence through every section of the Republic, and in war to endanger our independence.

The several States reserved the power at the formation of the Constitution to regulate and control titles and transfers of real property, and most, if not all, of them have laws disqualifying aliens from acquiring or holding lands within their limits. But this act, in disregard of the undoubted right of the States to prescribe such disqualifications, gives to alien stockholders in this bank an interest and title, as members of the corporation, to all the real property it may acquire within any of the States of this Union. This privilege granted to aliens is not *"necessary"* to enable the bank to perform its public duties, nor in any sense *"proper,"* because it is vitally subversive of the rights of the States.

The Government of the United States have no constitutional power to purchase lands within the States except "for the erection of forts, magazines, arsenals, dockyards, and

other needful buildings," and even for these objects only
"by the consent of the legislature of the State in which
the same shall be." By making themselves stockholders
in the bank and granting to the corporation the power to
purchase lands for other purposes they assume a power not
granted in the Constitution and grant to others what they
do not themselves possess. It is not *necessary* to the receiving, safe-keeping, or transmission of the funds of the
Government that the bank should possess this power, and
it is not *proper* that Congress should thus enlarge the powers delegated to them in the Constitution.

The old Bank of the United States possessed a capital of
only eleven millions of dollars, which was found fully sufficient to enable it with dispatch and safety to perform all
the functions required of it by the Government. The capital of the present bank is thirty-five millions of dollars, at
least twenty-four more than experience has proved to be
necessary to enable a bank to perform its public functions.
The public debt which existed during the period of the old
bank and on the establishment of the new has been nearly
paid off, and our revenue will soon be reduced. This increase of capital is therefore not for public, but for private
purposes.

The Government is the only *"proper"* judge where its
agents should reside and keep their offices, because it best
knows where their presence will be *"necessary."* It cannot, therefore, be *"necessary"* or *"proper"* to authorize the
bank to locate branches where it pleases to perform the
public service, without consulting the Government, and
contrary to its will. The principle laid down by the Supreme Court concedes that Congress cannot establish a
bank for purposes of private speculation and gain, but only

as a means of executing the delegated powers of the General Government. By the same principle a branch bank cannot constitutionally be established for other than public purposes. The power which this act gives to establish two branches in any State, without the injunction or request of the Government and for other than public purposes, is not *"necessary"* to the due *execution* of the powers delegated to Congress.

The bonus which is exacted from the bank is a confession upon the face of the act that the powers granted by it are greater than are *"necessary"* to its character of a fiscal agent. The Government does not tax its officers and agents for the privilege of serving it. The bonus of a million and a half required by the original charter and that of three millions proposed by this act are not exacted for the privilege of giving "the necessary facilities for transferring the public funds from place to place within the United States or the Territories thereof, and for distributing the same in payment of the public creditors without charging commission or claiming allowance on account of the difference of exchange," as required by the act of incorporation, but for something more beneficial to the stockholders. The original act declares that it (the bonus) is granted "in consideration of the exclusive privileges and benefits conferred by this act upon the said bank," and the act before me declares it to be "in consideration of the exclusive benefits and privileges continued by this act to the said corporation for fifteen years, as aforesaid." It is therefore for "exclusive privileges and benefits" conferred for their own use and emolument, and not for the advantage of the Government, that a bonus is exacted. These surplus powers for which the bank is required to pay cannot surely be *"necessary"* to make it the fiscal agent of the Treasury. If they were, the exaction of a bonus for them would not be *"proper."*

It is maintained by some that the bank is a means of executing the constitutional power "to coin money and regulate the value thereof." Congress have established a Mint to coin money and passed laws to regulate the value thereof. The money so coined, with its value so regulated, and such foreign coins as Congress may adopt are the only currency known to the Constitution. But if they have other power to regulate the currency, it was conferred to be exercised by themselves, and not to be transferred to a corporation. If the bank be established for that purpose, with a charter unalterable without its consent, Congress have parted with their power for a term of years, during which the Constitution is a dead letter. It is neither necessary nor proper to transfer its legislative power to such a bank, and therefore unconstitutional.

By its silence, considered in connection with the decision of the Supreme Court in the case of McCulloch against the State of Maryland, this act takes from the States the power to tax a portion of the banking business carried on within their limits, in subversion of one of the strongest barriers which secured them against Federal encroachments. Banking, like farming, manufacturing, or any other occupation or profession, is a *business,* the right to follow which is not originally derived from the laws. Every citizen and every company of citizens in all of our States possessed the right until the State Legislatures deemed it good policy to prohibit private banking by law. If the prohibitory State laws were now repealed, every citizen would again possess the right. The State banks are a qualified restoration of the right which has been taken away by the laws against banking, guarded by such provisions and limitations as in the opinion of the State Legislatures the public interest requires. These corporations, unless there be an exemption in their charter, are, like private bankers and banking companies, subject to State taxation. The manner in which these taxes shall be laid depends wholly on legislative discretion. It may be upon the bank, upon the stock, upon the profits, or in any other mode which the sovereign power shall will.

Upon the formation of the Constitution the States guarded their taxing power with peculiar jealousy. They surrendered it only as it regards imports and exports. In relation to every other object within their jurisdiction, whether persons, property, business, or professions, it was secured in as ample a manner as it was before possessed. All persons, though United States officers, are liable to a poll tax by the States within which they reside. The lands of the United States are liable to the usual land tax, except in the new States, from whom agreements that they will not tax unsold lands are exacted when they are admitted into the Union. Horses, wagons, any beasts or vehicles, tools, or property belonging to private citizens, though employed in the service of the United States, are subject to State taxation. Every private business, whether carried on by an officer of the General Government or not, whether it be mixed with public concerns or not, even if it be carried on by the Government of the United States itself, separately or in partnership, falls within the scope of the taxing power of the State. Nothing comes more fully within it than banks and the business of banking, by whomsoever instituted and carried on. Over this whole subject-matter it is just as absolute, unlimited, and uncontrollable as if the Constitution had never been adopted, because in the formation of that instrument it was reserved without qualification.

The principle is conceded that the States cannot rightfully tax the operations of the General Government. They cannot tax the money of the Government deposited in the State banks, nor the agency of those banks in remitting it; but will any man maintain that their mere selection to perform this public service for the General Government would exempt the State banks and their ordinary business from State taxation? Had the United States, instead of establishing a bank at Philadelphia, employed a private banker to keep and transmit their funds, would it have deprived Pennsylvania of the right to tax his bank and his usual banking operations? It will not be pretended. Upon what principle, then, are the banking establishments of the Bank of the United States and their usual banking operations to be exempted from taxation? It is not their public agency or the deposits of the Government which the States claim a right to tax, but their banks and their banking powers, instituted and exercised within State jurisdiction for their private emolument; those powers and privileges for which they pay a bonus, and which the States tax in their own banks. The exercise of these powers within a State, no matter by whom or under what authority, whether by private citizens in their original right, by corporate bodies created by the States, by foreigners or the agents of foreign governments located within their limits, forms a legitimate object of State taxation. From this and like sources, from the persons, property, and business that are found residing, located, or carried on under their jurisdiction, must the States, since the surrender of their right to raise a revenue from imports and exports, draw all the money necessary for the support of their governments and the maintenance of their independence. There is no more appropriate subject of taxation than banks, banking, and bank stocks, and none to which the States ought more pertinaciously to cling.

It cannot be *necessary* to the character of the bank as a fiscal agent of the Government that its private business should be exempted from that taxation to which all the State banks are liable, nor can I conceive it *"proper"* that the substantive and most essential powers reserved by the States shall be thus attacked and annihilated as a means of executing the powers delegated to the General Government. It may be safely assumed that none of those sages who had an agency in forming or adopting our Constitution ever imagined that any portion of the taxing power of the States not prohibited to them nor delegated to Congress was to be swept away and annihilated as a means of executing certain powers delegated to Congress.

If our power over means is so absolute that the Supreme Court will not call in question the constitutionality of an act of Congress the subject of which "is not prohibited, and is really calculated to effect any of the objects intrusted to the Government," although, as in the case before me, it takes away powers expressly granted to Congress and rights scrupulously reserved to the States, it becomes us to proceed in our legislation with the utmost caution. Though not directly, our own powers and the rights of the States may be indirectly legislated away in the use of means to execute substantive powers. We may not enact that Congress shall not have the power of exclusive legislation over the District of Columbia, but we may pledge the faith of the United States that as a means of executing other powers it shall not be exercised for twenty years or forever. We may not pass an act prohibiting the States to tax the banking business carried on within their limits, but we may, as a means of executing our powers over other objects, place that business in the hands of our agents and then declare it exempt from State taxation in their hands. Thus may our own powers and the rights of the States, which we cannot directly curtail or invade, be frittered away and extinguished in the use of means employed by us to execute other powers. That a bank of the United States, competent to all the duties which may be required by the Government, might be so organized as not to infringe on our own delegated powers or the reserved rights of the States I do not entertain a doubt. Had the Executive been called upon to furnish the project of such an institution, the duty would have been cheerfully performed. In the absence of such a call it was obviously proper that he should confine himself to pointing out those prominent features in the act presented which in his opinion make it incompatible with the Constitution and sound policy. A general discussion will now take place, eliciting new light and settling important principles; and a new Congress, elected in the midst of such discussion, and furnishing an equal representation of the people according to the last census, will bear to the Capitol the verdict of public opinion, and, I doubt not, bring this important question to a satisfactory result.

Under such circumstances the bank comes forward and asks a renewal of its charter for a term of fifteen years upon conditions which not only operate as a gratuity to the stockholders of many millions of dollars, but will sanction any abuses and legalize any encroachments.

Suspicions are entertained and charges are made of gross

abuse and violation of its charter. An investigation unwillingly conceded and so restricted in time as necessarily to make it incomplete and unsatisfactory discloses enough to excite suspicion and alarm. In the practices of the principal bank partially unveiled, in the absence of important witnesses, and in numerous charges confidently made and as yet wholly uninvestigated there was enough to induce a majority of the committee of investigation—a committee which was selected from the most able and honorable members of the House of Representatives—to recommend a suspension of further action upon the bill and a prosecution of the inquiry. As the charter had yet four years to run, and as a renewal now was not necessary to the successful prosecution of its business, it was to have been expected that the bank itself, conscious of its purity and proud of its character, would have withdrawn its application for the present, and demanded the severest scrutiny into all its transactions. In their declining to do so there seems to be an additional reason why the functionaries of the Government should proceed with less haste and more caution in the renewal of their monopoly.

The bank is professedly established as an agent of the executive branch of the Government, and its constitutionality is maintained on that ground. Neither upon the propriety of present action nor upon the provisions of this act was the Executive consulted. It has had no opportunity to say that it neither needs nor wants an agent clothed with such powers and favored by such exemptions. There is nothing in its legitimate functions which makes it necessary or proper. Whatever interest or influence, whether public or private, has given birth to this act, it cannot be found either in the wishes or necessities of the executive department, by which present action is deemed premature, and the powers conferred upon its agent not only unnecessary, but dangerous to the Government and country.

It is to be regretted that the rich and powerful too often bend the acts of government to their selfish purposes. Distinctions in society will always exist under every just government. Equality of talents, of education, or of wealth cannot be produced by human institutions. In the full enjoyment of the gifts of Heaven and the fruits of superior industry, economy, and virtue, every man is equally entitled to protection by law; but when the laws undertake to add to these natural and just advantages artificial distinctions, to grant titles, gratuities, and exclusive privileges, to make the rich richer and the potent more powerful, the humble members of society—the farmers, mechanics, and laborers—who have neither the time nor the means of securing like favors to themselves, have a right to complain of the injustice of their Government. There are no necessary evils in government. Its evils exist only in its abuses. If it would confine itself to equal protection, and, as Heaven does its rains, shower its favors alike on the high and the low, the rich and the poor, it would be an unqualified blessing. In the act before me there seems to be a wide and unnecessary departure from these just principles. . . .

Nor is our Government to be maintained or our Union preserved by invasions of the rights and powers of the several States. In thus attempting to make our General Government strong we make it weak. Its true strength consists in leaving individuals and States as much as possible to themselves; in making itself felt, not in its power, but in its beneficence; not in its control, but in its protection; not in binding the States more closely to the center, but leaving each to move unobstructed in its proper orbit.

Experience should teach us wisdom. Most of the difficulties our Government now encounters and most of the dangers which impend over our Union have sprung from an abandonment of the legitimate objects of Government by our national legislation, and the adoption of such principles as are embodied in this act. Many of our rich men have not been content with equal protection and equal benefits, but have besought us to make them richer by act of Congress. By attempting to gratify their desires we have in the results of our legislation arrayed section against section, interest against interest, and man against man, in a fearful commotion which threatens to shake the foundations of our Union. It is time to pause in our career to review our principles, and if possible revive that devoted patriotism and spirit of compromise which distinguished the sages of the Revolution and the fathers of our Union. If we cannot at once, in justice to interests vested under improvident legislation, make our Government what it ought to be, we can at least take a stand against all new grants of monopolies and exclusive privileges, against any prostitution of our Government to the advancement of the few at the expense of the many, and in favor of compromise and gradual reform in our code of laws and system of political economy.

I have now done my duty to my country. If sustained by my fellow-citizens, I shall be grateful and happy; if not, I shall find in the motives which impel me ample grounds for contentment and peace. In the difficulties which surround us and the dangers which threaten our institutions

there is cause for neither dismay nor alarm. For relief and
deliverance let us firmly rely on that kind Providence which
I am sure watches with peculiar care over the destinies of
our Republic, and on the intelligence and wisdom of our
countrymen. Through *His* abundant goodness and *their*
patriotic devotion our liberty and Union will be preserved.

Andrew Jackson

Washington, *July* 10, 1832

II. "The Safety of the Public Funds"

THIS memorandum, which was read to the
Cabinet on September 18, 1833, contains Jackson's reasons for the proposed withdrawal of the government's
deposits from the Second Bank of the United States.
In this statement Jackson reviews the arguments in
favor of his veto of the bill to recharter the bank, censures the bank for its policies since the veto, and dis-
cusses the constitutional issues involved in the removal
of the public deposits from the bank. Throughout the
struggle over the bank Jackson viewed himself as the
spokesman of the majority against a private institution
that was threatening both the economic rights of the
people and the continued existence of democratic government.

Reasons of the President*

READ TO THE CABINET ON THE 18TH OF SEPTEMBER, 1833

HAVING carefully and anxiously considered all the facts and
arguments which have been submitted to him relative to a
removal of the public deposits from the Bank of the United

---

* Reprinted from *Register of Debates in Congress*, 23 Congress, 1 Session, House, 1834, Vol. X, Appendix, pp. 284-289.

States, the President deems it his duty to communicate in this manner to his Cabinet the final conclusions of his own mind and the reasons on which they are founded, in order to put them in durable form and to prevent misconceptions.

The President's convictions of the dangerous tendencies of the Bank of the United States, since signally illustrated by its own acts, were so overpowering when he entered on the duties of Chief Magistrate that he felt it his duty, notwithstanding the objections of the friends by whom he was surrounded, to avail himself of the first occasion to call the attention of Congress and the people to the question of its recharter. The opinions expressed in his annual message of December, 1829, were reiterated in those of December, 1830 and 1831, and in that of 1830 he threw out for consideration some suggestions in relation to a substitute. At the session of 1831-'2 an act was passed by a majority of both Houses of Congress rechartering the present bank, upon which the President felt it his duty to put his constitutional veto. In his message returning that act he repeated and enlarged upon the principles and views briefly asserted in his annual message, declaring the bank to be, in his opinion, both inexpedient and unconstitutional, and announcing to his countrymen very unequivocally his firm determination never to sanction by his approval the continuance of that institution or the establishment of any other upon similar principles.

There are strong reasons for believing that the motive of the bank in asking for a recharter at that session of Congress was to make it a leading question in the election of a President of the United States the ensuing November, and all steps deemed necessary were taken to procure from the people a reversal of the President's decision.

Although the charter was approaching its termination, and the bank was aware that it was the intention of the Government to use the public deposit as fast as it has accrued in the payment of the public debt, yet did it extend its loans from January, 1831, to May, 1832, from $42,402,-304.24 to $70,428,070.72, being an increase of $28,025,-766.48 in sixteen months. It is confidently believed that the leading object of this immense extension of its loans was to bring as large a portion of the people as possible under its power and influence; and it has been disclosed that some of the largest sums were granted on very unusual terms to the conductors of the public press. In some of these cases the motive was made manifest by the nominal or insufficient security taken for the loans, by the large amounts discounted, by the extraordinary time allowed for payment, and especially by the subsequent conduct of those receiving the accommodations.

Having taken these preliminary steps to obtain control over public opinion, the bank came into Congress and asked a new charter. The object avowed by many of the advocates of the bank was to *put the President to the test,* that the country might know his final determination relative to the bank prior to the ensuing election. Many documents and articles were printed and circulated at the expense of the bank to bring the people to a favorable decision upon its pretensions. Those whom the bank appears to have made its debtors for the special occasion were warned of the ruin which awaited them should the President be sustained, and attempts were made to alarm the whole people by painting the depression in the price of property and produce and the general loss, inconvenience, and distress which it was represented would immediately follow the reelection of the President in opposition to the bank.

Can it now be said that the question of a recharter of the bank was not decided at the election which ensued? Had the veto been equivocal, or had it not covered the whole ground—if it had merely taken exceptions to the details of the bill or to the time of its passage—if it had not met the whole ground of constitutionality and expediency, then there might have been some plausibility for the allegation that the question was not decided by the people. It was to compel the President to take his stand that the question was brought forward at that particular time. He met the challenge, willingly took the position into which his adversaries sought to force him, and frankly declared his unalterable opposition to the bank as being both unconstitutional and inexpedient. On that ground the case was argued to the people, and now that the people have sustained the President, notwithstanding the array of influence and power which was brought to bear upon him, it is too late, he confidently thinks, to say that the question has not been decided. Whatever may be the opinions of others, the President considers his reelection as a decision of the people against the bank. In the concluding paragraph of his veto message he said:

I have now done my duty to my country. If sustained by my fellow-citizens, I shall be grateful and happy; if not, I shall find in the motives which impel me ample grounds for contentment and peace.

He was sustained by a just people, and he desires to evince his gratitude by carrying into effect their decision so far as it depends upon him.

Of all the substitutes for the present bank which have been suggested, none seems to have united any considerable portion of the public in its favor. Most of them are liable to the same constitutional objections for which the present bank has been condemned, and perhaps to all there are strong objections on the score of expediency. In ridding the country of an irresponsible power which has attempted to control the Government, care must be taken not to unite the same power with the Executive branch. To give a President the control over the currency and the power over individuals now possessed by the Bank of the United States, even with the material difference that he is responsible to the people, would be as objectionable and as dangerous as to leave it as it is. Neither one nor the other is necessary, and therefore ought not to be resorted to.

On the whole, the President considers it as conclusively settled that the charter of the Bank of the United States will not be renewed, and he has no reasonable ground to believe that any substitute will be established. Being bound to regulate his course by the laws as they exist, and not to anticipate the interference of the legislative power for the purpose of framing new systems, it is proper for him seasonably to consider the means by which the services rendered by the Bank of the United States are to be performed after its charter shall expire.

The existing laws declare that

the deposits of the money of the United States in places in which the said bank and branches thereof may be established shall be made in said bank or branches thereof unless the Secretary of the Treasury shall at any time otherwise order and direct, in which case the Secretary of the Treasury shall immediately lay before Congress, if in session, and, if not, immediately after the commencement of the next session, the reasons of such order or direction.

The power of the Secretary of the Treasury over the deposits is *unqualified*. The provision that he shall report his reasons to Congress is no limitation. Had it not been inserted he would have been responsible to Congress had he made a removal for any other than good reasons, and his responsibility now ceases upon the rendition of sufficient ones to Congress. The only object of the provision is to make his reasons accessible to Congress and enable that body the more readily to judge of their soundness and purity, and thereupon to make such further provision by law as the legislative power may think proper in relation to the deposit of the public money. Those reasons may be very diversified. It was asserted by the Secretary of the Treasury, without contradiction, as early as 1817, that he had power "to control the proceedings" of the Bank of the United States at any moment "by changing the deposits to the State banks" should it pursue an illiberal course toward those institutions; that "the Secretary of the Treasury will always be disposed to support the credit of the State banks, and will invariably direct transfers from the deposits of the public money in aid of their legitimate exertions to maintain their credit"; and he asserted a right to employ the State banks when the Bank of the United States should refuse to receive on deposit the notes of such State banks as the public interest required should be received in payment of the public dues. In several instances he did transfer the public deposits to State banks in the immediate vicinity of branches, for reasons connected only with the

safety of those banks, the public convenience, and the interests of the Treasury.

If it was lawful for Mr. Crawford, the Secretary of the
Treasury at that time, to act on these principles, it will be
difficult to discover any sound reason against the application of similar principles in still stronger cases. And it is a
matter of surprise that a power which in the infancy of the
bank was freely asserted as one of the ordinary and familiar
duties of the Secretary of the Treasury should now be
gravely questioned, and attempts made to excite and alarm
the public mind as if some new and unheard-of power was
about to be usurped by the executive branch of the Government.

It is but a little more than two and a half years to the
termination of the charter of the present bank. It is considered as the decision of the country that it shall then
cease to exist, and no man, the President believes, has reasonable ground for expectation that any other Bank of the
United States will be created by Congress. To the Treasury Department is intrusted the safe keeping and faithful
application of the public moneys. A plan of collection different from the present must therefore be introduced and
put in complete operation before the dissolution of the
present bank. When shall it be commenced? Shall no step
be taken in this essential concern until the charter expires
and the Treasury finds itself without an agent, its accounts
in confusion, with no depository for its funds, and the whole
business of the Government deranged? or shall it be de-
layed until six months, or a year, or two years before the
expiration of the charter? It is obvious that any new system which may be substituted in the place of the Bank
of the United States could not be suddenly carried into

effect on the termination of its existence without serious inconvenience to the Government and the people. Its vast amount of notes are then to be redeemed and withdrawn from circulation and its immense debt collected. These operations must be gradual, otherwise much suffering and distress will be brought upon the community. It ought to be not a work of months only, but of years, and the President thinks it cannot, with due attention to the interests of the people, be longer postponed. It is safer to begin it too soon than to delay it too long.

It is for the wisdom of Congress to decide upon the best substitute to be adopted in the place of the Bank of the United States; and the President would have felt himself relieved from a heavy and painful responsibility if in the charter to the bank Congress had reserved to itself the power of directing at its pleasure the public money to be elsewhere deposited, and had not devolved that power exclusively on one of the Executive Departments. It is useless now to inquire why this high and important power was surrendered by those who are peculiarly and appropriately the guardians of the public money. Perhaps it was an oversight. But as the President presumes that the charter to the bank is to be considered as a contract on the part of the Government, it is not now in the power of Congress to disregard its stipulations; and by the terms of that contract the public money is to be deposited in the bank during the continuance of its charter unless the Secretary of the Treasury shall otherwise direct. Unless, therefore, the Secretary of the Treasury first acts, Congress have no power over the subject, for they cannot add a new clause to the charter or strike one out of it without the consent of the bank; and consequently the public money must remain in

that institution to the last hour of its existence unless the
Secretary of the Treasury shall remove it at an earlier
day. The responsibility is thus thrown upon the Executive
branch of the Government of deciding how long before the
expiration of the charter the public interest will require the
deposits to be placed elsewhere. And although according
to the frame and principle of our Government this decision
would seem more properly to belong to the legislative
power, yet as the law has imposed it upon the Executive
department the duty ought to be faithfully and firmly met,
and the decision made and executed upon the best lights
that can be obtained and the best judgment that can be
formed. It would ill become the Executive branch of the
Government to shrink from any duty which the law im-
poses on it, to fix upon others the responsibility which justly
belongs to itself. And while the President anxiously wishes
to abstain from the exercise of doubtful powers and to
avoid all interference with the rights and duties of others,
he must yet with unshaken constancy discharge his own
obligations, and cannot allow himself to turn aside in order
to avoid any responsibility which the high trust with which
he has been honored requires him to encounter; and it being the duty of one of the Executive departments to decide
in the first instance, subject to the future action of the legislative power, whether the public deposits shall remain in
the Bank of the United States until the end of its existence
or be withdrawn some time before, the President has felt
himself bound to examine the question carefully and deliberately in order to make up his judgment on the subject,
and in his opinion the near approach of the termination of
the charter and the public considerations heretofore mentioned are of themselves amply sufficient to justify the re-

moval of the deposits, without reference to the conduct of the bank or their safety in its keeping.

But in the conduct of the bank may be found other reasons, very imperative in their character, and which require prompt action. Developments have been made from time to time of its faithlessness as a public agent, its misapplication of public funds, its interference in elections, its efforts by the machinery of committees to deprive the Government directors of a full knowledge of its concerns, and, above all, its flagrant misconduct as recently and unexpectedly disclosed in placing all the funds of the bank, including the money of the Government, at the disposition of the president of the bank, as means of operating upon public opinion and procuring a new charter, without requiring him to render a voucher for their disbursement. A brief recapitulation of the facts which justify these charges, and which have come to the knowledge of the public and the President, will, he thinks, remove every reasonable doubt as to the course which it is now the duty of the President to pursue.

We have seen that in sixteen months ending in May, 1832, the bank had extended its loans more than 28,000,000 dollars, although it knew the Government intended to appropriate most of its large deposit during that year in payment of the public debt. It was in May, 1832, that its loans arrived at the maximum, and in the preceding March so sensible was the bank that it would not be able to pay over the public deposit when it would be required by the Government that it commenced a secret negotiation, without the approbation or knowledge of the Government, with the agents for about $2,700,000 of the three per cent. stocks held in Holland, with a view of inducing them not to come forward for payment for one or more years after notice should be given by the Treasury Department. This arrangement would have enabled the bank to keep and use during that time the public money set apart for the payment of these stocks.

After this negotiation had commenced, the Secretary of the Treasury informed the bank that it was his intention to pay off one-half of the three per cents. on the first of the succeeding July, which amounted to about $6,500,000. The president of the bank, although the committee of investigation was then looking into its affairs at Philadelphia, came immediately to Washington, and upon representing that the bank was desirous of accommodating the importing merchants at New York (which it failed to do) and undertaking to pay the interest itself, procured the consent of the Secretary, after consultation with the President, to postpone the payment until the succeeding first of October.

Conscious that at the end of that quarter the bank would not be able to pay over the deposits and that further indulgence was not to be expected of the Government, an agent was dispatched to England secretly to negotiate with the holders of the public debt in Europe and induce them by the offer of an equal or higher interest than that paid by the Government to hold back their claims for one year, during which the bank expected thus to retain the use of $5,000,000 of the public money, which the Government should set apart for the payment of that debt. The agent made an arrangement on terms, in part, which were in direct violation of the charter of the bank; and when some incidents connected with this secret negotiation accidentally came to the knowledge of the public and the Government, then, and not before, so much of it as was palpably in violation of the charter was disavowed! A modification of the rest was attempted with the view of getting the certificates without payment of the money, and thus absolving the Government from its liability to the holders. In this scheme the bank was partially successful, but to this day the certificates of a portion of these stocks have not been paid and the bank retains the use of the money.

This effort to thwart the Government in the payment of the public debt that it might retain the public money to be used for their private interests, palliated by pretenses notoriously unfounded and insincere, would have justified the instant withdrawal of the public deposits. The negotiation itself rendered doubtful the ability of the bank to meet the demands of the Treasury, and the misrepresentations by which it was attempted to be justified proved that no reliance could be placed upon its allegations.

If the question of a removal of the deposits presented itself to the Executive in the same attitude that it appeared before the House of Representatives at their last session, their resolution in relation to the safety of the deposits would be entitled to more weight, although the decision of the question of removal has been confided by law to another department of the Government. But the question now occurs attended by other circumstances and new disclosures of the most serious import. It is true that in the message of the President which produced this inquiry and resolution on the part of the House of Representatives it was his object to obtain the aid of that body in making a thorough examination into the conduct and condition of the bank and its branches in order to enable the Executive department to decide whether the public money was longer safe in its hands. The limited power of the Secretary of the Treasury over the subject disabled him from making the investigation as fully and satisfactorily as it could be done by a committee of the House of Representatives, and hence the President desired the assistance of Congress to obtain for the Treasury Department a full knowledge of all the facts which were necessary to guide his judgment. But it was not his purpose, as the language of his message will show, to ask the representatives of the people to assume a responsibility which did not belong to them and relieve the Executive branch of the Government from the duty which the law had imposed upon it. It is due to the President that his object in that proceeding should be distinctly understood, and that he should acquit himself of all suspicion of seeking to escape from the performance of his own duties or of desiring to interpose another body between himself and the people in order to avoid a measure which he is called upon to meet. But although as an act of justice to himself he disclaims any design of soliciting the opinion of the House of Representatives in relation to his own duties in order to shelter himself from responsibility under the sanction of their counsel, yet he is at all times ready to listen to the suggestions of the representatives of the people, whether given voluntarily or upon solicitation, and to consider them with the profound respect to which all will admit that they are justly entitled. Whatever may be the consequences, however, to himself, he must finally form his own judgment where the Constitution and the law make it his duty to decide, and must act accordingly; and he is bound to suppose that such a course on his part will never be regarded by that elevated body as a mark of disrespect to itself; but that they will, on the contrary, esteem it the strongest evidence he can give of his fixed resolution conscientiously to discharge his duty to them and the country.

A new state of things has, however, arisen since the close of the last session of Congress, and evidence has since been laid before the President which he is persuaded would have led the House of Representatives to a different conclusion if it had come to their knowledge. The fact that the bank controls, and in some cases substantially *owns,* and by its money *supports* some of the leading presses of the country is now more clearly established. Editors to whom it loaned extravagant sums in 1831 and 1832, on unusual time and nominal security, have since turned out to be insolvent, and to others apparently in no better condition accommodations still more extravagant, on terms more unusual, and some without any security, have also been heedlessly granted.

The allegation which has so often circulated through these channels that the Treasury was bankrupt and the bank was sustaining it, when for many years there has not been less, on an average, than six millions of public money in that institution, might be passed over as a harmless misrepresentation; but when it is attempted by substantial acts to impair the credit of the Government and tarnish the honor of the country, such charges require more serious attention. With six millions of public money in its vaults, after having had the use of from five to twelve millions for nine years without interest, it became the purchaser of a bill drawn by our Government on that of France for about 900,000 dollars, being the first installment of the French indemnity. The purchase money was left in the use of the bank, being simply added to the Treasury deposit. The bank sold the bill in England, and the holder sent it to France for collection, and arrangements not having been made by the French Government for its payment, it was taken up by the agents of the bank in Paris with the funds of the bank in their hands. Under these circumstances it has through its organs openly assailed the credit of the Government, and has actually made and persists in a demand of fifteen per cent. or $158,842.77, as damages, when no damage, or none beyond some trifling expense, has in fact been sustained, and when the bank had in its own possession on deposit several millions of the public money which it was then using for its own profit. Is a fiscal agent of the Government, which thus seeks to enrich itself at the expense of the public, worthy of further trust?

There are other important facts not in the contemplation of the House of Representatives or not known to the members at the time they voted for the resolution.

Although the charter and the rules of the bank both declare that "not less than seven directors" shall be necessary to the transaction of business, yet the most important business, even that of granting discounts to any extent, is intrusted to a committee of five members, who do not report to the board.

To cut off all means of communication with the Government in relation to its most important acts at the commencement of the present year, not one of the Government directors was placed on any one committee. And although since, by an unusual remodeling of those bodies, some of those directors have been placed on some of the committees, they are yet entirely excluded from the committee of exchange, through which the greatest and most objectionable loans have been made.

When the Government directors made an effort to bring back the business of the bank to the board in obedience to the charter and the existing regulations, the board not only overruled their attempt, but altered the rule so as to make it conform to the practice, in direct violation of one of the most important provisions of the charter which gave them existence.

It has long been known that the president of the bank, by his single will, originates and executes many of the most important measures connected with the management and credit of the bank, and that the committee as well as the board of directors are left in entire ignorance of many acts done and correspondence carried on in their names, and apparently under their authority. The fact has been recently disclosed that an unlimited discretion has been and is now vested in the president of the bank to expend its funds in payment for preparing and circulating articles and purchasing pamphlets and newspapers, calculated by their contents to operate on elections and secure a renewal of its charter. It appears from the official report of the public directors that on the 30th November, 1830, the president submitted to the board an article published in the American Quarterly Review containing favorable notices of the bank, and suggested the expediency of giving it a wider circulation at the expense of the bank; whereupon the board passed the following resolution, viz:

Resolved, That the president be authorized to take such measures in regard to the circulation of the contents of the said article, either in whole or in part, as he may deem most for the interest of the bank.

By an entry in the minutes of the bank dated March 11, 1831, it appears that the president had not only caused a large edition of that article to be issued, but had also, be-

fore the resolution of 30th November was adopted, procured to be printed and widely circulated numerous copies
of the reports of General Smith and Mr. McDuffie in favor of the bank, and on that day he suggested the expediency of extending his power to the printing of other
articles which might subserve the purposes of the institution, whereupon the following resolution was adopted, viz:

Resolved, That the president is hereby authorized to
cause to be prepared and circulated such documents and
papers as may communicate to the people information in
regard to the nature and operations of the bank.

The expenditures purporting to have been made under
authority of these resolutions during the years 1831 and
1832 were about $80,000. For a portion of these expendi-
tures vouchers were rendered, from which it appears that
they were incurred in the purchase of some hundred thousand copies of newspapers, reports and speeches made in
Congress, reviews of the veto message and reviews of
speeches against the bank, etc. For another large portion
no vouchers whatever were rendered, but the various sums
were paid on orders of the president of the bank, making
reference to the resolution of the 11th of March, 1831.

On ascertaining these facts and perceiving that expenditures of a similar character were still continued, the Government directors a few weeks ago offered a resolution in
the board calling for a specific account of these expenditures, showing the objects to which they had been applied
and the persons to whom the money had been paid. This
reasonable proposition was voted down.

They also offered a resolution rescinding the resolutions

of November, 1830, and March, 1831. This also was re-jected.

Not content with thus refusing to recall the obnoxious power or even to require such an account of the expenditure as would show whether the money of the bank had in fact been applied to the objects contemplated by these resolutions, as obnoxious as they were, the board renewed the power already conferred, and even enjoined renewed attention to its exercise by adopting the following in lieu of the propositions submitted by the Government directors, viz:

Resolved, That the board have confidence in the wisdom and integrity of the president and in the propriety of the resolutions of 30th November, 1830, and 11th March, 1831, and entertain a full conviction of the necessity of a renewed attention to the object of those resolutions, and that the president be authorized and requested to continue his exertions for the promotion of said object.

Taken in connection with the nature of the expenditures heretofore made, as recently disclosed, which the board not only tolerate, but approve, this resolution puts the funds of the bank at the disposition of the president for the purpose of employing the whole press of the country in the service of the bank, to hire writers and newspapers, and to pay out such sums as he pleases to what person and for what services he pleases without the responsibility of rendering any specific account. The bank is thus converted into a vast electioneering engine, with means to embroil the country in deadly feuds, and, under cover of expenditures, in themselves improper, extend its corruption through all the ramifications of society.

Some of the items for which accounts have been rendered show the construction which has been given to the resolutions and the way in which the power it confers has been exerted. The money has not been expended merely in the publication and distribution of speeches, reports of committees, or articles written for the purpose of showing the constitutionality or usefulness of the bank, but publications have been prepared and extensively circulated containing the grossest invectives against the officers of the Government; and the money which belongs to the stockholders and to the public has been freely applied in efforts to degrade in public estimation those who were supposed to be instrumental in resisting the wishes of this grasping and dangerous institution. As the president of the bank has not been required to settle his accounts, no one but himself knows how much more than the sum already mentioned may have been squandered, and for which a credit may hereafter be claimed in his account under this most extraordinary resolution. With these facts before us can we be surprised at the torrent of abuse incessantly poured out against all who are supposed to stand in the way of the cupidity or ambition of the Bank of the United States? Can we be surprised at sudden and unexpected changes of opinion in favor of an institution which has millions to lavish and avows its determination not to spare its means when they are necessary to accomplish its purposes? The refusal to render an account of the manner in which a part of the money expended has been applied gives just cause for the suspicion that it has been used for purposes which it is not deemed prudent to expose to the eyes of an intelligent and virtuous people. Those who act justly do not shun the light, nor do they refuse explanations when the propriety of their conduct is brought into question.

With these facts before him in an official report from the Government directors, the President would feel that he was not only responsible for all the abuses and corruptions the bank has committed or may commit, but almost an accomplice in a conspiracy against that Government which he has sworn honestly to administer, if he did not take every step within his constitutional and legal power likely to be efficient in putting an end to these enormities. If it be possible within the scope of human affairs to find a reason for removing the Government deposits and leaving the bank to its own resource for the means of effecting its criminal designs, we have it here. Was it expected, when the moneys of the United States were directed to be placed in that bank, that they would be put under the control of one man empowered to spend millions without rendering a voucher or specifying the object? Can they be considered safe with the evidence before us that tens of thousands have been spent for highly improper if not corrupt purposes, and that the same motive may lead to the expenditure of hundreds of thousands, and even millions, more? And can we justify ourselves to the people by longer lending to it the money and power of the Government to be employed for such purposes?

It has been alleged by some as an objection to the removal of the deposits that the bank has the power, and in that event will have the disposition, to destroy the State banks employed by the Government, and bring distress upon the country. It has been the fortune of the President to encounter dangers which were represented as equally alarming, and he has seen them vanish before resolution and energy. Pictures equally appalling were paraded before him when this bank came to demand a new charter. But what was the result? Has the country been ruined, or even distressed? Was it ever more prosperous than since that act? The President verily believes the bank has not the power to produce the calamities its friends threaten. The funds of the Government will not be annihilated by being transferred. They will immediately be issued for the benefit of trade; and if the Bank of the United States curtails its loans the State banks, strengthened by the public deposits, will extend theirs. What comes in through one bank will go out through others, and the equilibrium will be preserved. Should the bank, for the mere purpose of producing distress, press its debtors more heavily than some of them can bear, the consequences will recoil upon itself, and in the attempts to embarrass the country it will only bring loss and ruin upon the holders of its own stock. But if the President believed the bank possessed all the power which has been attributed to it, his determination would only be rendered the more inflexible. If, indeed, this corporation now holds in its hands the happiness and prosperity of the American people, it is high time to take the alarm. If the despotism be already upon us and our only safety is in the mercy of the despot, recent developments in relation to his designs and the means he employs show how necessary it is to shake it off. The struggle can never come with less distress to the people or under more favorable auspices than at the present moment.

All doubt as to the willingness of the State banks to undertake the service of the Government to the same extent and on the same terms as it is now performed by the

Bank of the United States is put to rest by the report of
the agent recently employed to collect information, and
from that willingness their own safety in the operation
may be confidently inferred. Knowing their own resources
better than they can be known by others, it is not to be
supposed that they would be willing to place themselves
in a situation which they cannot occupy without danger
of annihilation or embarrassment. The only consideration
applies to the safety of the public funds if deposited in
those institutions, and when it is seen that the directors of
many of them are not only willing to pledge the character
and capital of the corporations in giving success to this
measure, but also their own property and reputation, we
cannot doubt that they at least believe the public deposits
would be safe in their management. The President thinks
that these facts and circumstances afford as strong a guarantee as can be had in human affairs for the safety of the
public funds and the practicability of a new system of collection and disbursement through the agency of the State
banks.

From all these considerations the President thinks that
the State banks ought immediately to be employed in the
collection and disbursement of the public revenue, and the
funds now in the Bank of the United States drawn out with
all convenient dispatch. The safety of the public moneys
if deposited in the State banks must be secured beyond all
reasonable doubts; but the extent and nature of the security, in addition to their capital, if any be deemed necessary,
is a subject of detail to which the Treasury Department will
undoubtedly give its anxious attention. The banks to be
employed must remit the moneys of the Government without charge, as the Bank of the United States now does; must

render all the services which that bank now performs; must keep the Government advised of their situation by periodical returns; in fine, in any arrangement with the State banks the Government must not in any respect be placed on a worse footing than it now is. The President is happy to perceive by the report of the agent that the banks which he has consulted have, in general, consented to perform the service on these terms, and that those in New York have further agreed to make payments in London without other charge than the mere cost of the bills of exchange.

It should also be enjoined upon any banks which may be employed that it will be expected of them to facilitate domestic exchanges for the benefit of internal commerce; to grant all reasonable facilities to the payers of the revenue; to exercise the utmost liberality toward the other State banks, and do nothing uselessly to embarrass the Bank of the United States.

As one of the most serious objections to the Bank of the United States is the power which it concentrates, care must be taken in finding other agents for the service of the Treasury not to raise up another power equally formidable. Although it would probably be impossible to produce such a result by any organization of the State banks which could be devised—yet it is desirable to avoid even the appearance. To this end it would be expedient to assume no more power over them and interfere no more in their affairs than might be absolutely necessary to the security of the public deposit and the faithful performance of their duties as agents of the Treasury. Any interference by them in the political contests of the country with a view to influence elections ought, in the opinion of the President, to be followed by an immediate discharge from the public service.

It is the desire of the President that the control of the banks and the currency shall as far as possible be entirely separated from the political power of the country as well as wrested from an institution which has already attempted to subject the Government to its will. In his opinion the action of the General Government on this subject ought not to extend beyond the grant in the Constitution, which only authorizes Congress "to coin money and regulate the value thereof"; all else belongs to the States and the people, and must be regulated by public opinion and the interests of trade.

In conclusion, the President must be permitted to remark that he looks upon the pending question as of higher consideration than the mere transfer of a sum of money from one bank to another. Its decision may affect the character of our Government for ages to come. Should the bank be suffered longer to use the public moneys in the accomplishment of its purposes, with the proofs of its faithlessness and corruption before our eyes, the patriotic among our citizens will despair of success in struggling against its power, and we shall be responsible for entailing it upon our country forever. Viewing it as a question of transcendent importance, both in the principles and consequences it involves, the President could not, in justice to the responsibility which he owes to the country, refrain from pressing upon the Secretary of the Treasury his view of the considerations which impel to immediate action. Upon him has been devolved by the Constitution and the suffrages of the American people the duty of superintending the operation of the Executive Departments of the Government and seeing that the laws are faithfully executed. In the performance of this high trust it is his undoubted right to express to those whom the laws and his own choice have made his associates in the administration of the Government his opinion of their duties under circumstances as they arise. It is this right which he now exercises. Far be it from him to expect or require that any member of the Cabinet should at his request, order, or dictation do any act which he believes unlawful or in his conscience condemns. From them and from his fellow-citizens in general he desires only that aid and support which their reason approves and their conscience sanctions.

In the remarks he has made on this all-important question he trusts the Secretary of the Treasury will see only the frank and respectful declarations of the opinions which the President has formed on a measure of great national interest deeply affecting the character and usefulness of his Administration, and not a spirit of dictation, which the President would be as careful to avoid as ready to resist. Happy will he be if the facts now disclosed produce uniformity of opinion and unity of action among the members of the Administration.

The President again repeats that he begs his Cabinet to consider the proposed measure as his own, in the support of which he shall require no one of them to make a sacrifice of opinion or principle. Its responsibility has been assumed after the most mature deliberation and reflection as necessary to preserve the morals of the people, the freedom of the press, and the purity of the elective franchise, without which all will unite in saying that the blood and treasure expended by our forefathers in the establishment of our happy system of government will have been vain and fruitless. Under these convictions he feels that a measure so important to the American people cannot be commenced too soon; and he therefore names the first day of October next as a period proper for the change of the deposits, or sooner, provided the necessary arrangements with the State banks can be made.

Andrew Jackson

III. "The Rapid Increase of a Spurious Currency"

After the withdrawal of the public deposits from the Second Bank of the United States, Jackson became increasingly alarmed over the inflationary effects of the notes issued by every variety of bank. As early as 1817 he had opposed the paper-money party in Tennessee, and as President he repeatedly proposed that "a larger portion of the precious metals" be "infused into our circulating medium." In the following excerpt from the annual message of 1836, Jackson summarizes his views on the dangers of paper money and on the advantages of "a currency consisting of the precious metals."

Message*

*Fellow-Citizens of the Senate and
House of Representatives:*

. . . I beg leave to call your attention to another subject . . . the currency of the country.

It is apparent from the whole context of the Constitution, as well as the history of the times which gave birth to it, that it was the purpose of the convention to establish

---

* Reprinted from *Executive Documents*, 24 Congress, 2 Session, 1836, Vol. I, Doc. No. 2, pp. 11-14.

a currency consisting of the precious metals. These, from their peculiar properties which rendered them the standard of value in all other countries, were adopted in this as well to establish its commercial standard in reference to foreign countries by a permanent rule as to exclude the use of a mutable medium of exchange, such as of certain agricultural commodities recognized by the statutes of some States as a tender for debts, or the still more pernicious expedient of a paper currency. The last, from the experience of the evils of the issues of paper during the Revolution, had become so justly obnoxious as not only to suggest the clause in the Constitution forbidding the emission of bills of credit by the States, but also to produce that vote in the Convention which negatived the proposition to grant power to Congress to charter corporations, a proposition well understood at the time as intended to authorize the establishment of a national bank, which was to issue a currency of bank notes on a capital to be created to some extent out of Government stocks. Although this proposition was refused by a direct vote of the convention, the object was afterwards in effect obtained by its ingenious advocates through a strained construction of the Constitution. The debts of the Revolution were funded at prices which formed no equivalent compared with the nominal amount of the stock, and under circumstances which exposed the motives of some of those who participated in the passage of the act to distrust.

The facts that the value of the stock was greatly enhanced by the creation of the bank, that it was well understood that such would be the case, and that some of the advocates of the measure were largely benefited by it belong to the history of the times, and are well calculated to diminish the respect which might otherwise have been due to the action of the Congress which created the institution.

On the establishment of a national bank it became the interest of its creditors that gold should be superseded by the paper of the bank as a general currency. A value was soon attached to the gold coins which made their exportation to foreign countries as a mercantile commodity more profitable than their retention and use at home as money. It followed as a matter of course, if not designed by those who established the bank, that the bank became in effect a substitute for the mint of the United States.

Such was the origin of a national bank currency, and such the beginning of those difficulties which now appear in the excessive issues of the banks incorporated by the various States.

Although it may not be possible by any legislative means within our power to change at once the system which has thus been introduced, and has received the acquiescence of all portions of the country, it is certainly our duty to do all that is consistent with our constitutional obligations in preventing the mischiefs which are threatened by its undue extension. That the efforts of the fathers of our Government to guard against it by a constitutional provision were founded on an intimate knowledge of the subject has been frequently attested by the bitter experience of the country. The same causes which led them to refuse their sanction to a power authorizing the establishment of incorporations for banking purposes now exist in a much stronger degree to urge us to exert the utmost vigilance in calling into action the means necessary to correct the evils resulting from the unfortunate exercise of the power, and it is to be hoped that the opportunity for effecting this great good will be improved before the country witnesses new scenes of embarrassment and distress.

Variableness must ever be the characteristic of a currency of which the precious metals are not the chief ingredient, or which can be expanded or contracted without regard to the principles that regulate the value of those metals as a standard in the general trade of the world. With us bank issues constitute such a currency, and must ever do so until they are made dependent on those just proportions of gold and silver as a circulating medium which experience has proved to be necessary not only in this but in all other commercial countries. Where those proportions are not infused into the circulation and do not control it, it is manifest that prices must vary according to the tide of bank issues, and the value and stability of property must stand exposed to all the uncertainty which attends the administration of institutions that are constantly liable to the temptation of an interest distinct from that of the community in which they are established.

The progress of an expansion, or rather a depreciation, of the currency by excessive bank issues is always attended by a loss to the laboring classes. This portion of the community have neither time nor opportunity to watch the ebbs and flows of the money market. Engaged from day to day in their useful toils, they do not perceive that although their wages are nominally the same, or even somewhat higher, they are greatly reduced in fact by the rapid increase of a spurious currency, which, as it appears to make money abound, they are at first inclined to consider a blessing. It is not so with the speculator, by whom this operation is better understood, and is made to contribute to his advantage. It is not until the prices of the necessaries

of life become so dear that the laboring classes cannot supply their wants out of their wages that the wages rise and
gradually reach a justly proportioned rate to that of the
products of their labor. When thus, by the depreciation in
consequence of the quantity of paper in circulation, wages
as well as prices become exorbitant, it is soon found that
the whole effect of the adulteration is a tariff on our home
industry for the benefit of the countries where gold and
silver circulate and maintain uniformity and moderation in
prices. It is then perceived that the enhancement of the
price of land and labor produces a corresponding increase
in the price of products until these products do not sustain
a competition with similar ones in other countries, and thus
both manufactured and agricultural productions cease to
bear exportation from the country of the spurious currency,
because they cannot be sold for cost. This is the process
by which specie is banished by the paper of the banks.
Their vaults are soon exhausted to pay for foreign commodities; the next step is a stoppage of specie payment—a
total degradation of paper as a currency—unusual depression of prices, the ruin of debtors, and the accumulation of
property in the hands of creditors and cautious capitalists.

It was in view of these evils, together with the dangerous
power wielded by the Bank of the United States and its
repugnance to our Constitution, that I was induced to exert
the power conferred upon me by the American people to
prevent the continuance of that institution. But although
various dangers to our republican institutions have been
obviated by the failure of that bank to extort from the Government a renewal of its charter, it is obvious that little
has been accomplished except a salutary change of public
opinion toward restoring to the country the sound currency

provided for in the Constitution. In the acts of several of
the States prohibiting the circulation of small notes, and
the auxiliary enactments of Congress at the last session forbidding their reception or payment on public account, the
true policy of the country has been advanced and a larger
portion of the precious metals infused into our circulating
medium. These measures will probably be followed up in
due time by the enactment of State laws banishing from
circulation bank notes of still higher denominations, and
the object may be materially promoted by further acts of
Congress forbidding the employment as fiscal agents of
such banks as continue to issue notes of low denominations
and throw impediments in the way of the circulation of
gold and silver.

The effects of an extension of bank credits and overissues
of bank paper have been strikingly illustrated in the sales
of the public lands. From the returns made by the various
Registers and Receivers in the early part of last summer
it was perceived that the receipts arising from the sales
of the public lands were increasing to an unprecedented
amount. In effect, however, these receipts amounted to
nothing more than credits in bank. The banks lent out their
notes to speculators. They were paid to the Receivers and
immediately returned to the banks, to be lent out again
and again, being mere instruments to transfer to speculators the most valuable public land and pay the Government
by a credit on the books of the banks. Those credits on
the books of some of the Western banks, usually called deposits, were already greatly beyond their immediate means
of payment, and were rapidly increasing. Indeed, each
speculation furnished means for another; for no sooner had
one individual or company paid in the notes than they were

immediately lent to another for a like purpose, and the banks were extending their business and their issues so largely as to alarm considerate men and render it doubtful whether these bank credits if permitted to accumulate would ultimately be of the least value to the Government. The spirit of expansion and speculation was not confined to the deposit banks, but pervaded the whole multitude of banks throughout the Union and was giving rise to new institutions to aggravate the evil.

The safety of the public funds and the interest of the people generally required that these operations should be checked; and it became the duty of every branch of the General and State Governments to adopt all legitimate and proper means to produce that salutary effect. Under this view of my duty I directed the issuing of the order which will be laid before you by the Secretary of the Treasury, requiring payment for the public lands sold to be made in specie, with an exception until the 15th of the present month in favor of actual settlers. This measure has produced many salutary consequences. It checked the career of the Western banks and gave them additional strength in anticipation of the pressure which has since pervaded our Eastern as well as the European commercial cities. By preventing the extension of the credit system it measurably cut off the means of speculation and retarded its progress in monopolizing the most valuable of the public lands. It has tended to save the new States from a nonresident proprietorship, one of the greatest obstacles to the advancement of a new country and the prosperity of an old one. It has tended to keep open the public lands for entry by emigrants at Government prices instead of their being compelled to purchase of speculators at double or triple prices.

And it is conveying into the interior large sums in silver and gold, there to enter permanently into the currency of the country and place it on a firmer foundation. It is confidently believed that the country will find in the motives which induced that order and the happy consequences which will have ensued much to commend and nothing to condemn. . . .

Andrew Jackson

Washington, *5th December,* 1836

VII · The Powers of the President

I. "The President Is the Direct Represent-
ative of the American People"

AT THE INSTIGATION of Henry Clay, the Senate in 1834 adopted a resolution censuring Jackson for the Secretary of the Treasury's removal of the Federal deposits from the Second Bank of the United States. Jackson replied to the vote of censure with a "solemn protest" in which he alternately defended his own acts and attacked those of the Senate. The "Protest," which the Senate refused to enter in its "Journal," is the most sweeping and straightforward defense of the Presidential powers ever made by a chief executive of the United States.

Protest*

To the Senate of the United States:

IT APPEARS by the published Journal of the Senate that on the 26th of December last a resolution was offered by a member of the Senate, which after a protracted debate was on the 28th day of March last modified by the mover and

---

* Reprinted from *Register of Debates in Congress,* 23 Congress, 1 Session, Senate, 1833-1834, Vol. X, pp. 1317-1336.

passed by the votes of twenty-six Senators out of forty-six who were present and voted, in the following words, viz:

Resolved, That the President, in the late Executive proceedings in relation to the public revenue, has assumed upon himself authority and power not conferred by the Constitution and laws, but in derogation of both.

Having had the honor, through the voluntary suffrages of the American people, to fill the office of President of the United States during the period which may be presumed to have been referred to in this resolution, it is sufficiently evident that the censure it inflicts was intended for myself. Without notice, unheard and untried, I thus find myself charged on the records of the Senate, and in a form hitherto unknown in our history, with the high crime of violating the laws and Constitution of my country.

It can seldom be necessary for any department of the Government, when assailed in conversation or debate or by the strictures of the press or of popular assemblies, to step out of its ordinary path for the purpose of vindicating its conduct or of pointing out any irregularity or injustice in the manner of the attack. But when the chief Executive Magistrate is, by one of the most important branches of the Government in its official capacity, in a public manner, and by its recorded sentence, but without precedent, competent authority, or just cause, declared guilty of a breach of the laws and Constitution, it is due to his station, to public opinion, and to a proper self-respect that the officer thus denounced should promptly expose the wrong which has been done.

In the present case, moreover, there is even a stronger

necessity for such a vindication. By an express provision of the Constitution, before the President of the United States can enter on the execution of his office he is required to take an oath or affirmation in the following words:

I do solemnly swear (or affirm) that I will faithfully execute the office of President of the United States and will to the best of my ability preserve, protect, and defend the Constitution of the United States.

The duty of defending, so far as in him lies, the integrity of the Constitution would indeed have resulted from the very nature of his office; but by thus expressing it in the official oath or affirmation, which in this respect differs from that of any other functionary, the founders of our Republic have attested their sense of its importance and have given to it a peculiar solemnity and force. Bound to the performance of this duty by the oath I have taken, by the strongest obligations of gratitude to the American people, and by the ties which unite my every earthly interest with the welfare and glory of my country, and perfectly convinced that the discussion and passage of the above-mentioned resolution were not only unauthorized by the Constitution, but in many respects repugnant to its provisions and subversive of the rights secured by it to other co-ordinate departments, I deem it an imperative duty to maintain the supremacy of that sacred instrument and the immunities of the department intrusted to my care by all means consistent with my own lawful powers, with the rights of others, and with the genius of our civil institutions. To this end I have caused this my solemn protest against the aforesaid proceedings to be placed on the files of the Executive department and to be transmitted to the Senate.

It is alike due to the subject, the Senate, and the people that the views which I have taken of the proceedings referred to, and which compel me to regard them in the light that has been mentioned, should be exhibited at length, and with the freedom and firmness which are required by an occasion so unprecedented and peculiar.

Under the Constitution of the United States the powers and functions of the various departments of the Federal Government and their responsibilities for violation or neglect of duty are clearly defined or result by necessary inference. The legislative power, subject to the qualified negative of the President, is vested in the Congress of the United States, composed of the Senate and House of Representatives. The executive power is vested exclusively in the President, except that in the conclusion of treaties and in certain appointments to office he is to act with the advice and consent of the Senate. The judicial power is vested exclusively in the Supreme and other courts of the United States, except in cases of impeachment, for which purpose the accusatory power is vested in the House of Representatives and that of hearing and determining in the Senate. But although for the special purposes which have been mentioned there is an occasional intermixture of the powers of the different departments, yet with these exceptions each of the three great departments is independent of the others in its sphere of action; and when it deviates from that sphere is not responsible to the others further than it is expressly made so in the Constitution. In every other respect each of them is the coequal of the other two, and all are the servants of the American people, without power or right to control or censure each other in the service of their common superior, save only in the manner and to the degree which that superior has prescribed.

The responsibilities of the President are numerous and weighty. He is liable to impeachment for high crimes and misdemeanors, and on due conviction to removal from office and perpetual disqualification; and notwithstanding such conviction, he may also be indicted and punished according to law. He is also liable to the private action of any party who may have been injured by his illegal mandates or instructions in the same manner and to the same extent as the humblest functionary. In addition to the responsibilities which may thus be enforced by impeachment, criminal prosecution, or suit at law, he is also accountable at the bar of public opinion for every act of his administration. Subject only to the restraints of truth and justice, the free people of the United States have the undoubted right, as individuals or collectively, orally or in writing, at such times and in such language and form as they may think proper, to discuss his official conduct and to express and promulgate their opinions concerning it. Indirectly also his conduct may come under review in either branch of the legislature, or in the Senate when acting in its executive capacity, and so far as the executive or legislative proceedings of these bodies may require it, it may be exercised by them. These are believed to be the proper and only modes in which the President of the United States is to be held accountable for his official conduct.

Tested by these principles, the resolution of the Senate is wholly unauthorized by the Constitution, and in derogation of its entire spirit. It assumes that a single branch of the legislative department may for the purposes of a public censure, and without any view to legislation or impeachment, take up, consider, and decide upon the official acts of the Executive. But in no part of the Constitution is the President subjected to any such responsibility, and in no part of that instrument is any such power conferred on either branch of the legislature.

The justice of these conclusions will be illustrated and confirmed by a brief analysis of the powers of the Senate and a comparison of their recent proceedings with those powers.

The high functions assigned by the Constitution to the Senate are in their nature either legislative, executive, or judicial. It is only in the exercise of its judicial powers, when sitting as a court for the trial of impeachments, that the Senate is expressly authorized and necessarily required to consider and decide upon the conduct of the President or any other public officer. Indirectly, however, as has already been suggested, it may frequently be called on to perform that office. Cases may occur in the course of its legislative or executive proceedings in which it may be indispensable to the proper exercise of its powers that it should inquire into and decide upon the conduct of the President or other public officers; and in every such case its constitutional right to do so is cheerfully conceded. But to authorize the Senate to enter on such a task in its legislative or executive capacity, the inquiry must actually grow out of and tend to some legislative or executive action, and the decision, when expressed, must take the form of some appropriate legislative or executive act.

The resolution in question was introduced, discussed, and passed not as a joint but as a separate resolution. It asserts no legislative power, proposes no legislative action, and neither possesses the form nor any of the attributes of a legislative measure. It does not appear to have been entertained or passed with any view or expectation of its issuing in a law or joint resolution, or in the repeal of any law or joint resolution, or in any other legislative action.

Whilst wanting both the form and substance of a legislative measure, it is equally manifest that the resolution was not justified by any of the executive powers conferred on the Senate. These powers relate exclusively to the consideration of treaties and nominations to office; and they are exercised in secret session and with closed doors. This resolution does not apply to any treaty or nomination, and was passed in a public session.

Nor does this proceeding in any way belong to that class of incidental resolutions which relate to the officers of the Senate, to their Chamber and other appurtenances, or to subjects of order and other matters of the like nature—in all which either House may lawfully proceed without any co-operation with the other or with the President.

On the contrary, the whole phraseology and sense of the resolution seem to be judicial. Its essence, true character, and only practical effect are to be found in the conduct which it charges upon the President and in the judgment which it pronounces on that conduct. The resolution, therefore, though discussed and adopted by the Senate in its legislative capacity, is in its office and in all its characteristics essentially judicial.

That the Senate possesses a high judicial power and that instances may occur in which the President of the United States will be amenable to it is undeniable. But under the provisions of the Constitution it would seem to be equally plain that neither the President nor any other officer can be rightfully subjected to the operation of the judicial power of the Senate except in the cases and under the forms prescribed by the Constitution.

The Constitution declares that "the President, Vice President, and all civil officers of the United States shall be removed from office on impeachment for and conviction of treason, bribery, or other high crimes and misdemeanors"; that the House of Representatives "shall have the sole power of impeachment"; that the Senate "shall have the sole power to try all impeachments"; that "when sitting for that purpose they shall be on oath or affirmation"; that "when the President of the United States is tried the Chief Justice shall preside"; that "no person shall be convicted without the concurrence of two-thirds of the members present," and that "judgment shall not extend further than to removal from office and disqualification to hold and enjoy any office of honor, trust, or profit under the United States."

The resolution above quoted charges, in substance, that in certain proceedings relating to the public revenue the President has usurped authority and power not conferred upon him by the Constitution and laws, and that in doing so he violated both. Any such act constitutes a high crime—one of the highest, indeed, which the President can commit—a crime which justly exposes him to impeachment by the House of Representatives, and, upon due conviction, to removal from office and to the complete and immutable disfranchisement prescribed by the Constitution.

The resolution, then, was in substance an impeachment of the President, and in its passage amounts to a declaration by a majority of the Senate that he is guilty of an impeachable offense. As such it is spread upon the journals of the Senate, published to the nation and to the world, made part of our enduring archives, and incorporated in the history of the age. The punishment of removal from office and future disqualification does not, it is true, follow this decision, nor would it have followed the like decision if the regular forms of proceeding had been pursued, because the requisite number did not concur in the result. But the moral influence of a solemn declaration by a majority of the Senate that the accused is guilty of the offense charged upon him has been as effectually secured as if the like declaration had been made upon an impeachment expressed in the same terms. Indeed, a greater practical effect has been gained, because the votes given for the resolution, though not sufficient to authorize a judgment of guilty on an impeachment, were numerous enough to carry that resolution.

That the resolution does not expressly allege that the assumption of power and authority which it condemns was intentional and corrupt is no answer to the preceding view of its character and effect. The act thus condemned necessarily implies volition and design in the individual to whom it is imputed, and, being unlawful in its character, the legal conclusion is that it was prompted by improper motives and committed with an unlawful intent. The charge is not of a mistake in the exercise of supposed powers, but of the assumption of powers not conferred by the Constitution and laws, but in derogation of both, and nothing is suggested to excuse or palliate the turpitude of the act. In the absence of any such excuse or palliation there is only room for one inference, and that is that the intent was unlawful and corrupt. Besides, the resolution not only contains no mitigating suggestions, but, on the contrary, it holds up the act complained of as justly obnoxious to censure and reprobation, and thus as distinctly stamps it with impurity of motive as if the strongest epithets had been used.

The President of the United States, therefore, has been by a majority of his constitutional triers accused and found guilty of an impeachable offense; but in no part of this proceeding have the directions of the Constitution been observed.

The impeachment, instead of being preferred and prosecuted by the House of Representatives, originated in the Senate, and was prosecuted without the aid or concurrence of the other House. The oath or affirmation prescribed by the Constitution was not taken by the Senators, the Chief Justice did not preside, no notice of the charge was given to the accused, and no opportunity afforded him to respond to the accusation, to meet his accusers face to face, to cross-examine the witnesses, to procure counteracting testimony, or to be heard in his defense. The safeguards and formalities which the Constitution has connected with the power of impeachment were doubtless supposed by the framers of that instrument to be essential to the protection of the public servant, to the attainment of justice, and to the order, impartiality, and dignity of the procedure. These safeguards and formalities were not only practically disregarded in the commencement and conduct of these proceedings, but in their result I find myself convicted by less than two-thirds of the members present of an impeachable offense.

In vain may it be alleged in defense of this proceeding that the form of the resolution is not that of an impeachment or of a judgment thereupon, that the punishment prescribed in the Constitution does not follow its adoption, or that in this case no impeachment is to be expected from the House of Representatives. It is because it did not assume the form of an impeachment that it is the more palpably repugnant to the Constitution, for it is through that form only that the President is judicially responsible to the Senate; and though neither removal from office nor future disqualification ensues, yet it is not to be presumed that the framers of the Constitution considered either or both of those results as constituting the whole of the punishment they prescribed. The judgment of guilty by the highest tribunal in the Union, the stigma it would inflict on the offender, his family, and fame, and the perpetual record on the Journal, handing down to future generations the story of his disgrace, were doubtless regarded by them as the bitterest portions, if not the very essence, of that punishment. So far, therefore, as some of its most material parts are concerned, the passage, recording, and promulgation of the resolution are an attempt to bring them on the President in a manner unauthorized by the Constitution. To shield him and other officers who are liable to impeachment from consequences so momentous, except when really merited by official delinquencies, the Constitution has most carefully guarded the whole process of impeachment. A majority of the House of Representatives must think the officer guilty before he can be charged. Two-thirds of the Senate must pronounce him guilty or he is deemed to be innocent. Forty-six Senators appear by the Journal to have been present when the vote on the resolution was taken. If after all the solemnities of an impeachment thirty of those Senators had voted that the President was guilty, yet would he have been acquitted; but by the mode of proceeding adopted in the present case a lasting record of conviction has been entered up by the votes of twenty-six Senators without an impeachment or trial, whilst the Constitution expressly declares that to the entry of such a judgment an accusation by the House of Representatives, a trial by the Senate, and a concurrence of two-thirds in the vote of guilty shall be indispensable prerequisites.

Whether or not an impeachment was to be expected from the House of Representatives was a point on which the Senate had no constitutional right to speculate, and in respect to which, even had it possessed the spirit of prophecy, its anticipations would have furnished no just ground for this procedure. Admitting that there was reason to believe that a violation of the Constitution and laws had been actually committed by the President, still it was the duty of the Senate, as his sole constitutional judges, to wait for an impeachment until the other House should think proper to prefer it. The members of the Senate could have no right to infer that no impeachment was intended. On the contrary, every legal and rational presumption on their part ought to have been that if there was good reason to believe him guilty of an impeachable offense the House of Representatives would perform its constitutional duty by arraigning the offender before the justice of his country. The contrary presumption would involve an implication derogatory to the integrity and honor of the representatives of the people. But suppose the suspicion thus implied were actually entertained and for good cause, how can it justify the assumption by the Senate of powers not conferred by the Constitution?

It is only necessary to look at the condition in which the Senate and the President have been placed by this proceeding to perceive its utter incompatibility with the provisions and the spirit of the Constitution and with the plainest dictates of humanity and justice.

If the House of Representatives shall be of opinion that there is just ground for the censure pronounced upon the President, then will it be the solemn duty of that House to prefer the proper accusation and to cause him to be brought to trial by the constitutional tribunal. But in what condition would he find that tribunal? A majority of its members have already considered the case, and have not only formed but expressed a deliberate judgment upon its merits. It is the policy of our benign systems of jurisprudence to secure in all criminal proceedings, and even in the most trivial litigations, a fair, unprejudiced, and impartial trial. And surely it cannot be less important that such a trial should be secured to the highest officer of the Government.

The Constitution makes the House of Representatives the exclusive judges, in the first instance, of the question whether the President has committed an impeachable offense. A majority of the Senate, whose interference with this preliminary question has for the best of all reasons been studiously excluded, anticipate the action of the House of Representatives, assume not only the function which belongs exclusively to that body, but convert themselves into accusers, witnesses, counsel, and judges, and prejudge the whole case, thus presenting the appalling spectacle in a free state of judges going through a labored preparation for an impartial hearing and decision by a previous *ex parte* investigation and sentence against the supposed offender.

There is no more settled axiom in that Government whence we derived the model of this part of our Constitu-

tion than that "the lords cannot impeach any to themselves, nor join in the accusation, because they are judges."
Independently of the general reasons on which this rule
is founded, its propriety and importance are greatly increased by the nature of the impeaching power. The power
of arraigning the high officers of government before a tribunal whose sentence may expel them from their seats and
brand them as infamous is eminently a popular remedy—a
remedy designed to be employed for the protection of private right and public liberty against the abuses of injustice
and the encroachments of arbitrary power. But the framers
of the Constitution were also undoubtedly aware that this
formidable instrument had been and might be abused, and
that from its very nature an impeachment for high crimes
and misdemeanors, whatever might be its result, would in
most cases be accompanied by so much of dishonor and
reproach, solicitude and suffering, as to make the power
of preferring it one of the highest solemnity and importance. It was due to both these considerations that the
impeaching power should be lodged in the hands of those
who from the mode of their election and the tenure of their
offices would most accurately express the popular will and
at the same time be most directly and speedily amenable
to the people. The theory of these wise and benignant
intentions is in the present case effectually defeated by the
proceedings of the Senate. The members of that body represent not the people, but the States; and though they are
undoubtedly responsible to the States, yet from their extended term of service the effect of that responsibility during the whole period of that term must very much depend
upon their own impressions of its obligatory force. When
a body thus constituted expresses beforehand its opinion

in a particular case, and thus indirectly invites a prosecution, it not only assumes a power intended for wise reasons to be confined to others, but it shields the latter from that exclusive and personal responsibility under which it was intended to be exercised, and reverses the whole scheme of this part of the Constitution.

Such would be some of the objections to this procedure, even if it were admitted that there is just ground for imputing to the President the offenses charged in the resolution. But if, on the other hand, the House of Representatives shall be of opinion that there is no reason for charging them upon him, and shall therefore deem it improper to prefer an impeachment, then will the violation of privilege as it respects that House, of justice as it regards the President, and of the Constitution as it relates to both be only the more conspicuous and impressive.

The constitutional mode of procedure on an impeachment has not only been wholly disregarded, but some of the first principles of natural right and enlightened jurisprudence have been violated in the very form of the resolution. It carefully abstains from averring in which of "the late proceedings in relation to the public revenue the President has assumed upon himself authority and power not conferred by the Constitution and laws." It carefully abstains from specifying what laws or what parts of the Constitution have been violated. Why was not the certainty of the offense—"the nature and cause of the accusation"—set out in the manner required in the Constitution before even the humblest individual, for the smallest crime, can be exposed to condemnation? Such a specification was due to the accused that he might direct his defense to the real points of attack, to the people that they might clearly under-

stand in what particulars their institutions had been violated, and to the truth and certainty of our public annals.
As the record now stands, whilst the resolution plainly
charges upon the President at least one act of usurpation in
"the late Executive proceedings in relation to the public
revenue," and is so framed that those Senators who believed
that one such act, and only one, had been committed could
assent to it, its language is yet broad enough to include several such acts, and so it may have been regarded by some of
those who voted for it. But though the accusation is thus
comprehensive in the censures it implies, there is no such
certainty of time, place, or circumstance as to exhibit the
particular conclusion of fact or law which induced any one
Senator to vote for it. And it may well have happened that
whilst one Senator believed that some particular act embraced in the resolution was an arbitrary and unconstitutional assumption of power, others of the majority may have
deemed that very act both constitutional and expedient, or,
if not expedient, yet still within the pale of the Constitution.
And thus a majority of the Senators may have been enabled
to concur in a vague and undefined accusation that the President, in the course of "the late Executive proceedings in
relation to the public revenue," had violated the Constitution and laws, whilst if a separate vote had been taken in
respect to each particular act included within the general
terms the accusers of the President might on any such vote
have been found in the minority.

Still further to exemplify this feature of the proceeding,
it is important to be remarked that the resolution, as originally offered to the Senate, specified with adequate precision certain acts of the President which it denounced as a
violation of the Constitution and laws, and that it was not

until the very close of the debate, and when perhaps it was apprehended that a majority might not sustain the specific accusation contained in it, that the resolution was so modified as to assume its present form. A more striking illustration of the soundness and necessity of the rules which forbid vague and indefinite generalities and require a reasonable certainty in all judicial allegations, and a more glaring instance of the violation of those rules, has seldom been exhibited.

In this view of the resolution it must certainly be regarded not as a vindication of any particular provision of the law or the Constitution, but simply as an official rebuke or condemnatory sentence, too general and indefinite to be easily repelled, but yet sufficiently precise to bring into discredit the conduct and motives of the Executive. But whatever it may have been intended to accomplish, it is obvious that the vague, general, and abstract form of the resolution is in perfect keeping with those other departures from first principles and settled improvements in jurisprudence so properly the boast of free countries in modern times. And it is not too much to say of the whole of these proceedings that if they shall be approved and sustained by an intelligent people, then will that great contest with arbitrary power which had established in statutes, in bills of rights, in sacred charters, and in constitutions of government the right of every citizen to a notice before trial, to a hearing before conviction, and to an impartial tribunal for deciding on the charge have been waged in vain.

If the resolution had been left in its original form, it is not to be presumed that it could ever have received the assent of a majority of the Senate, for the acts therein specified as violations of the Constitution and laws were clearly within the limits of the Executive authority. They are the "dismissing the late Secretary of the Treasury because he would not, contrary to his sense of his own duty, remove the money of the United States in deposit with the Bank of the United States and its branches in conformity with the President's opinion, and appointing his successor to effect such removal, which has been done." But as no other specification has been substituted, and as these were the "Executive proceedings in relation to the public revenue" principally referred to in the course of the discussion, they will doubtless be generally regarded as the acts intended to be denounced as "an assumption of authority and power not conferred by the Constitution or laws, but in derogation of both." It is therefore due to the occasion that a condensed summary of the views of the Executive in respect to them should be here exhibited.

By the Constitution "the executive power is vested in a President of the United States." Among the duties imposed upon him, and which he is sworn to perform, is that of "taking care that the laws be faithfully executed." Being thus made responsible for the entire action of the executive department, it was but reasonable that the power of appointing, overseeing, and controlling those who execute the laws—a power in its nature executive—should remain in his hands. It is therefore not only his right, but the Constitution makes it his duty, to "nominate and, by and with the advice and consent of the Senate, appoint" all "officers of the United States whose appointments are not in the Constitution otherwise provided for," with a proviso that the appointment of inferior officers may be vested in the President alone, in the courts of justice, or in the heads of Departments.

The executive power vested in the Senate is neither that of "nominating" nor "appointing." It is merely a check upon the Executive power of appointment. If individuals are proposed for appointment by the President by them deemed incompetent or unworthy, they may withhold their consent and the appointment cannot be made. They check the action of the Executive, but cannot in relation to those very subjects act themselves nor direct him. Selections are still made by the President, and the negative given to the Senate, without diminishing his responsibility, furnishes an additional guarantee to the country that the subordinate executive as well as the judicial offices shall be filled with worthy and competent men.

The whole executive power being vested in the President, who is responsible for its exercise, it is a necessary consequence that he should have a right to employ agents of his own choice to aid him in the performance of his duties, and to discharge them when he is no longer willing to be responsible for their acts. In strict accordance with this principle, the power of removal, which, like that of appointment, is an original executive power, is left unchecked by the Constitution in relation to all executive officers, for whose conduct the President is responsible, while it is taken from him in relation to judicial officers, for whose acts he is not responsible. In the government from which many of the fundamental principles of our system are derived the head of the executive department originally had power to appoint and remove at will all officers, executive and judicial. It was to take the judges out of this general power of removal, and thus make them independent of the Executive, that the tenure of their offices was changed to good behavior. Nor is it conceivable why they are placed in our

Constitution upon a tenure different from that of all other officers appointed by the Executive unless it be for the same purpose.

But if there were any just ground for doubt on the face of the Constitution whether all executive officers are removable at the will of the President, it is obviated by the cotemporaneous construction of the instrument and the uniform practice under it.

The power of removal was a topic of solemn debate in the Congress of 1789 while organizing the administrative departments of the Government, and it was finally decided that the President derived from the Constitution the power of removal so far as it regards that department for whose acts he is responsible. Although the debate covered the whole ground, embracing the Treasury as well as all the other Executive Departments, it arose on a motion to strike out of the bill to establish a Department of Foreign Affairs, since called the Department of State, a clause declaring the Secretary "to be removable from office by the President of the United States." After that motion had been decided in the negative it was perceived that these words did not convey the sense of the House of Representatives in relation to the true source of the power of removal. With the avowed object of preventing any future inference that this power was exercised by the President in virtue of a grant from Congress, when in fact that body considered it as derived from the Constitution, the words which had been the subject of debate were struck out, and in lieu thereof a clause was inserted in a provision concerning the chief clerk of the Department, which declared that "whenever the said principal officer shall be removed from office by the President of the United States, or in any other case of vacancy," the chief clerk should during such vacancy have charge of the papers of the office. This change having been made for the express purpose of declaring the sense of Congress that the President derived the power of removal from the Constitution, the act as it passed has always been considered as a full expression of the sense of the legislature on this important part of the American Constitution.

Here then we have the concurrent authority of President Washington, of the Senate, and the House of Representatives, numbers of whom had taken an active part in the convention which framed the Constitution and in the State conventions which adopted it, that the President derived an unqualified power of removal from that instrument itself, which is "beyond the reach of legislative authority." Upon this principle the Government has now been steadily administered for about forty-five years, during which there have been numerous removals made by the President or by his direction, embracing every grade of executive officers from the heads of departments to the messengers of bureaus.

The Treasury Department in the discussions of 1789 was considered on the same footing as the other executive departments, and in the act establishing it were incorporated the precise words indicative of the sense of Congress that the President derives his power to remove the Secretary from the Constitution, which appear in the act establishing the Department of Foreign Affairs. An assistant Secretary of the Treasury was created, and it was provided that he should take charge of the books and papers of the department "whenever the Secretary shall be removed from office by the President of the United States." The Secretary of the Treasury being appointed by the President, and being considered as constitutionally removable by him, it appears never to have occurred to anyone in the Congress of 1789, or since until very recently, that he was other than an executive officer, the mere instrument of the Chief Magistrate in the execution of the laws, subject, like all other heads of departments, to his supervision and control. No such idea as an officer of the Congress can be found in the Constitution or appears to have suggested itself to those who organized the Government. There are officers of each House the appointment of which is authorized by the Constitution, but all officers referred to in that instrument as coming within the appointing power of the President, whether established thereby or created by law, are "officers of the United States." No joint power of appointment is given to the two Houses of Congress, nor is there any accountability to them as one body; but as soon as any office is created by law, of whatever name or character, the appointment of the person or persons to fill it devolves by the Constitution upon the President, with the advice and consent of the Senate, unless it be an inferior office, and the appointment be vested by the law itself "in the President alone, in the courts of law, or in the heads of departments."

But at the time of the organization of the Treasury Department, an incident occurred which distinctly evinces the unanimous concurrence of the first Congress in the principle that the Treasury Department is wholly executive in its character and responsibilities. A motion was made to strike out the provision of the bill making it the duty of the Secretary "to digest and report plans for the improvement and management of the revenue and for the support of public credit," on the ground that it would give the executive department of the Government too much influence and power in Congress. The motion was not opposed on the ground that the Secretary was the officer of Congress and responsible to that body, which would have been conclusive if admitted, but on other ground, which conceded his executive character throughout. The whole discussion evinces an unanimous concurrence in the principle that the Secretary of the Treasury is wholly an executive officer, and the struggle of the minority was to restrict his power as such. From that time down to the present the Secretary of the Treasury, the Treasurer, Register, Comptrollers, Auditors, and Clerks who fill the offices of that Department have in the practice of the Government been considered and treated as on the same footing with corresponding grades of officers in all the other executive departments.

The custody of the public property, under such regulations as may be prescribed by legislative authority, has always been considered an appropriate function of the executive department in this and all other Governments. In accordance with this principle, every species of property belonging to the United States (excepting that which is in the use of the several co-ordinate departments of the Government as means to aid them in performing their appropriate functions) is in charge of officers appointed by the President, whether it be lands, or buildings, or merchandise, or provisions, or clothing, or arms and munitions of war. The superintendents and keepers of the whole are appointed by the President, responsible to him, and removable at his will.

Public money is but a species of public property. It cannot be raised by taxation or customs, nor brought into the Treasury in any other way except by law; but whenever or howsoever obtained, its custody always has been and always must be, unless the Constitution, be changed, intrusted to the executive department. No officer can be created by Congress for the purpose of taking charge of it whose appointment would not by the Constitution at once devolve on the President and who would not be responsible to him for the faithful performance of his duties. The legislative power may undoubtedly bind him and the President by any laws they may think proper to enact; they may prescribe in what place particular portions of the public property shall be kept and for what reason it shall be removed, as they may direct that supplies for the Army or Navy shall be kept in particular stores, and it will be the duty of the President to see that the law is faithfully executed—yet will the custody remain in the executive department of the Government. Were the Congress to assume, with or without a legislative act, the power of appointing officers, independently of the President, to take the charge and custody of the public property contained in the military and naval arsenals, magazines, and storehouses, it is believed that such an act would be regarded by all as a palpable usurpation of executive power, subversive of the form as well as the fundamental principles of our Government. But where is the difference in principle whether the public property be in the form of arms, munitions of war, and supplies or in gold and silver or bank notes? None can be perceived—none is believed to exist. Congress cannot, therefore, take out of the hands of the executive department the custody of the public property or money without an assumption of executive power and a subversion of the first principles of the Constitution.

The Congress of the United States have never passed

an act imperatively directing that the public moneys shall be kept in any particular place or places. From the origin of the Government to the year 1816 the statute-book was wholly silent on the subject. In 1789 a Treasurer was created, subordinate to the Secretary of the Treasury, and through him to the President. He was required to give bond safely to keep and faithfully to disburse the public moneys, without any direction as to the manner or places in which they should be kept. By reference to the practice of the Government it is found that from its first organization the Secretary of the Treasury, acting under the supervision of the President, designated the places in which the public moneys should be kept, and especially directed all transfers from place to place. This practice was continued, with the silent acquiescence of Congress, from 1789 down to 1816, and although many banks were selected and discharged, and although a portion of the moneys were first placed in the State banks, and then in the former Bank of the United States, and upon the dissolution of that were again transferred to the State banks, no legislation was thought necessary by Congress, and all the operations were originated and perfected by executive authority. The Secretary of the Treasury, responsible to the President, and with his approbation, made contracts and arrangements in relation to the whole subject-matter, which was thus entirely committed to the direction of the President under his responsibilities to the American people and to those who were authorized to impeach and punish him for any breach of this important trust.

The act of 1816 establishing the Bank of the United States directed the deposits of public money to be made in that bank and its branches in places in which the said bank and branches thereof may be established, "unless the Secretary of the Treasury should otherwise order and direct," in which event he was required to give his reasons to Congress. This was but a continuation of his pre-existing power as the head of an executive department to direct where the deposits should be made, with the superadded obligation of giving his reasons to Congress for making them elsewhere than in the Bank of the United States and its branches. It is not to be considered that this provision in any degree altered the relation between the Secretary of the Treasury and the President as the responsible head of the executive department, or released the latter from his constitutional obligation to "take care that the laws be faithfully executed." On the contrary, it increased his responsibilities by adding another to the long list of laws which it was his duty to carry into effect.

It would be an extraordinary result if because the person charged by law with a public duty is one of his Secretaries it were less the duty of the President to see that law faithfully executed than other laws enjoining duties upon subordinate officers or private citizens. If there be any difference, it would seem that the obligation is the stronger in relation to the former, because the neglect is in his presence and the remedy at hand.

It cannot be doubted that it was the legal duty of the Secretary of the Treasury to order and direct the deposits of the public money to be made elsewhere than in the Bank of the United States whenever sufficient reasons existed for making the change. If in such a case he neglected or refused to act, he would neglect or refuse to execute the law. What would be the sworn duty of the President? Could he say that the Constitution did not bind him to see the law faithfully executed because it was one of his Secretaries and not himself upon whom the service was specially imposed? Might he not be asked whether there was any such limitation to his obligations prescribed in the Constitution—whether he is not equally bound to take care that the laws be faithfully executed, whether they impose duties on the highest officer of State or the lowest subordinate in any of the Departments? Might he not be told that it was for the sole purpose of causing all executive officers, from the highest to the lowest, faithfully to perform the services required of them by law—that the people of the United States have made him their Chief Magistrate and the Constitution has clothed him with the entire executive power of this Government? The principles implied in these questions appear too plain to need elucidation.

But here also we have a cotemporaneous construction of the act which shows that it was not understood as in any way changing the relations between the President and Secretary of the Treasury, or as placing the latter out of Executive control even in relation to the deposits of the public money. Nor on this point are we left to any equivocal testimony. The documents of the Treasury Department show that the Secretary of the Treasury did apply to the President and obtained his approbation and sanction to the original transfer of the public deposits to the present Bank of the United States, and did carry the measure into effect in obedience to his decision. They also show that transfers of the public deposits from the branches of the Bank of the United States to State banks at Chillicothe, Cincinnati, and Louisville, in 1819, were made with the approbation of the President and by his authority. They show that upon all important questions appertaining to his Department,

whether they related to the public deposits or other matters, it was the constant practice of the Secretary of the
Treasury to obtain for his acts the approval and sanction
of the President. These acts and the principles on which
they were founded were known to all the departments of
the Government, to Congress and the country, and until
very recently appear never to have been called in question.

Thus was it settled by the Constitution, the laws, and
the whole practice of the Government that the entire executive power is vested in the President of the United
States; that as incident to that power the right of appointing and removing those officers who are to aid him
in the execution of the laws, with such restrictions only
as the Constitution prescribes, is vested in the President;
that the Secretary of the Treasury is one of those officers;
that the custody of the public property and money is an
executive function which, in relation to the money, has
always been exercised through the Secretary of the Treasury and his subordinates; that in the performance of these
duties he is subject to the supervision and control of the
President, and in all important measures having relation
to them consults the Chief Magistrate and obtains his approval and sanction; that the law establishing the bank did
not, as it could not, change the relation between the President and the Secretary—did not release the former from
his obligation to see the law faithfully executed nor the
latter from the President's supervision and control; that
afterwards and before the Secretary did in fact consult and
obtain the sanction of the President to transfers and removals of the public deposits, and that all departments of
the Government, and the nation itself, approved or ac-

quiesced in these acts and principles as in strict conformity with our Constitution and laws.

During the last year the approaching termination, according to the provisions of its charter and the solemn decision of the American people, of the Bank of the United States made it expedient, and its exposed abuses and corruptions made it, in my opinion, the duty of the Secretary of the Treasury, to place the moneys of the United States in other depositories. The Secretary did not concur in that opinion, and declined giving the necessary order and direction. So glaring were the abuses and corruptions of the bank, so evident its fixed purpose to persevere in them, and so palpable its design by its money and power to control the Government and change its character, that I deemed it the imperative duty of the executive authority, by the exertion of every power confided to it by the Constitution and laws, to check its career and lessen its ability to do mischief, even in the painful alternative of dismissing the head of one of the departments. At the time the removal was made other causes sufficient to justify it existed, but if they had not the Secretary would have been dismissed for this cause only.

His place I supplied by one whose opinions were well known to me, and whose frank expression of them in another situation and generous sacrifices of interest and feeling when unexpectedly called to the station he now occupies ought forever to have shielded his motives from suspicion and his character from reproach. In accordance with the views long before expressed by him he proceeded, with my sanction, to make arrangements for depositing the moneys of the United States in other safe institutions.

The resolution of the Senate as originally framed and as passed, if it refers to these acts, pre-supposes a right in that body to interfere with this exercise of Executive power. If the principle be once admitted, it is not difficult to perceive where it may end. If by a mere denunciation like this resolution the President should ever be induced to act in a matter of official duty contrary to the honest convictions of his own mind in compliance with the wishes of the Senate, the constitutional independence of the executive department would be as effectually destroyed and its power as effectually transferred to the Senate as if that end had been accomplished by an amendment of the Constitution. But if the Senate have a right to interfere with the Executive powers, they have also the right to make that interference effective; and if the assertion of the power implied in the resolution be silently acquiesced in we may reasonably apprehend that it will be followed at some future day by an attempt at actual enforcement. The Senate may refuse, except on the condition that he will surrender his opinions to theirs and obey their will, to perform their own constitutional functions, to pass the necessary laws, to sanction appropriations proposed by the House of Representatives, and to confirm proper nominations made by the President. It has already been maintained (and it is not conceivable that the resolution of the Senate can be based on any other principle) that the Secretary of the Treasury is the officer of Congress and independent of the President; that the President has no right to control him, and consequently none to remove him. With the same propriety and on similar grounds may the Secretary of State, the Secretaries of War and the Navy, and the Postmaster General each in succession be declared independent of the President, the subordinates of Congress, and removable only with the concurrence of the Senate. Followed to its consequences, this principle will be found effectually to destroy one co-ordinate department of the Government, to concentrate in the hands of the Senate the whole executive power, and to leave the President as powerless as he would be useless—the shadow of authority after the substance had departed.

The time and the occasion which have called forth the resolution of the Senate seem to impose upon me an additional obligation not to pass it over in silence. Nearly forty-five years had the President exercised, without a question as to his rightful authority, those powers for the recent assumption of which he is now denounced. The vicissitudes of peace and war had attended our Government; violent parties, watchful to take advantage of any seeming usurpation on the part of the Executive, had distracted our councils; frequent removals, or forced resignations in every sense tantamount to removals, had been made of the Secretary and other officers of the Treasury, and yet in no one instance is it known that any man, whether patriot or partisan, had raised his voice against it as a violation of the Constitution. The expediency and justice of such changes in reference to public officers of all grades have frequently been the topic of discussion, but the constitutional right of the President to appoint, control, and remove the head of the Treasury as well as all other Departments seems to have been universally conceded. And what is the occasion upon which other principles have been first officially asserted? The Bank of the United States, a great moneyed monopoly, had attempted to obtain a renewal of its charter by controlling the elections of the people and the action of the Government. The use of its corporate funds and power in that attempt was fully disclosed, and it was made known to the President that the corporation was putting in train the same course of measures, with the view of making another vigorous effort, through an interference in the elections of the people, to control public opinion and force the Government to yield to its demands. This, with its corruption of the press, its violation of its charter, its exclusion of the Government directors from its proceedings, its neglect of duty and arrogant pretensions, made it, in the opinion of the President, incompatible with the public interest and the safety of our institutions that it should be longer employed as the fiscal agent of the Treasury. A Secretary of the Treasury appointed in the recess of the Senate, who had not been confirmed by that body, and whom the President might or might not at his pleasure nominate to them, refused to do what his superior in the executive department considered the most imperative of his duties, and became in fact, however innocent his motives, the protector of the bank. And on this occasion it is discovered for the first time that those who framed the Constitution misunderstood it; that the first Congress and all its successors have been under a delusion; that the practice of near forty-five years is but a continued usurpation; that the Secretary of the Treasury is not responsible to the President, and that to remove him is a violation of the Constitution and laws for which the President deserves to stand forever dishonored on the journals of the Senate.

There are also some other circumstances connected with the discussion and passage of the resolution to which I feel it to be not only my right, but my duty, to refer. It appears by the Journal of the Senate that among the twenty-six Senators who voted for the resolution on its final passage, and who had supported it in debate in its original form, were one of the Senators from the State of Maine, the two Senators from New Jersey, and one of the Senators from Ohio. It also appears by the same Journal and by the files of the Senate that the legislatures of these States had severally expressed their opinions in respect to the Executive proceedings drawn in question before the Senate.

The two branches of the legislature of the State of Maine on the 25th of January, 1834, passed a preamble and series of resolutions in the following words:

Whereas at an early period after the election of Andrew Jackson to the Presidency, in accordance with the sentiments which he had uniformly expressed, the attention of Congress was called to the constitutionality and expediency of the renewal of the charter of the United States Bank; and whereas the bank has transcended its chartered limits in the management of its business transactions, and has abandoned the object of its creation by engaging in political controversies, by wielding its power and influence to embarrass the Administration of the General Government, and by bringing insolvency and distress upon the commercial community; and whereas the public security from such an institution consists less in its present pecuniary capacity to discharge its liabilities than in the fidelity with which the trusts reposed in it have been executed; and whereas the abuse and misapplication of the powers conferred have destroyed the confidence of the public in the officers of the bank and demonstrated that such powers endanger the stability of republican institutions: Therefore,

Resolved, That in the removal of the public deposits from the Bank of the United States, as well as in the manner of their removal, we recognize in the Administration an adherence to constitutional rights and the performance of a public duty.

Resolved, That this legislature entertain the same opinion as heretofore expressed by preceding legislatures of this State, that the Bank of the United States ought not to be rechartered.

Resolved, That the Senators of this State in the Congress of the United States be instructed and the Representatives be requested to oppose the restoration of the deposits and the renewal of the charter of the United States Bank.

On the 11th of January, 1834, the house of assembly and council composing the legislature of the State of New Jersey passed a preamble and a series of resolutions in the following words:

Whereas the present crisis in our public affairs calls for a decided expression of the voice of the people of this State; and whereas we consider it the undoubted right of the legislatures of the several States to instruct those who represent their interests in the councils of the nation in all matters which intimately concern the public weal and may affect the happiness or well-being of the people: Therefore,

1. *Be it resolved by the council and general assembly of this State,* That while we acknowledge with feelings of devout gratitude our obligations to the Great Ruler of Nations for His mercies to us as a people that we have been preserved alike from foreign war, from the evils of internal commotions, and the machinations of designing and ambitious men who would prostrate the fair fabric of our Union, that we ought nevertheless to humble ourselves in His presence and implore His aid for the perpetuation of our republican institutions and for a continuance of that unexampled prosperity which our country has hitherto enjoyed.

2. *Resolved,* That we have undiminished confidence in the integrity and firmness of the venerable patriot who now holds the distinguished post of Chief Magistrate of this nation, and whose purity of purpose and elevated motives have so often received the unqualified approbation of a large majority of his fellow-citizens.

3. *Resolved,* That we view with agitation and alarm the existence of a great moneyed incorporation which threatens to embarrass the operations of the Government and by means of its unbounded influence upon the currency of the country to scatter distress and ruin throughout the community, and that we therefore solemnly believe the present Bank of the United States ought not to be rechartered.

4. *Resolved,* That our Senators in Congress be instructed and our members of the House of Representatives be requested to sustain, by their votes and influence, the course adopted by the Secretary of the Treasury, Mr. Taney, in relation to the Bank of the United States and the deposits of the Government moneys, believing as we do the course of the Secretary to have been constitutional, and that the public good required its adoption.

5. *Resolved,* That the governor be requested to forward a copy of the above resolutions to each of our Senators and Representatives from this State to the Congress of the United States.

On the 21st day of February last the legislature of the same State reiterated the opinions and instructions before given by joint resolutions in the following words:

Resolved by the council and general assembly of the State of New Jersey, That they do adhere to the resolutions passed by them on the 11th day of January last, relative to the President of the United States, the Bank of the United States, and the course of Mr. Taney in removing the Government deposits.

Resolved, That the legislature of New Jersey have not seen any reason to depart from such resolutions since the passage thereof, and it is their wish that they should receive from our Senators and Representatives of this State in the Congress of the United States that attention and obedience which are due to the opinion of a sovereign State openly expressed in its legislative capacity.

On the 2d of January, 1834, the senate and house of representatives composing the legislature of Ohio passed a preamble and resolutions in the following words:

Whereas there is reason to believe that the Bank of the United States will attempt to obtain a renewal of its charter at the present session of Congress; and whereas it is abundantly evident that said bank has exercised powers derogatory to the spirit of our free institutions and dangerous to the liberties of these United States; and whereas there is just reason to doubt the constitutional power of Congress to grant acts of incorporation for banking purposes out of the District of Columbia; and whereas we believe the proper disposal of the public lands to be of the utmost importance to the people of these United States, and that honor and good faith require their equitable distribution:

Therefore,

Resolved by the general assembly of the State of Ohio, That we consider the removal of the public deposits from the Bank of the United States as required by the best interests of our country, and that a proper sense of public duty imperiously demanded that that institution should be no longer used as a depository of the public funds.

Resolved also, That we view with decided disapprobation the renewed attempts in Congress to secure the passage of the bill providing for the disposal of the public domain upon the principles proposed by Mr. Clay, inasmuch as we believe that such a law would be unequal in its operations and unjust in its results.

Resolved also, That we heartily approve of the principles set forth in the late veto message upon that subject; and

Resolved, That our Senators in Congress be instructed and our Representatives requested to use their influence to prevent the rechartering of the Bank of the United States, to sustain the Administration in its removal of the public deposits, and to oppose the passage of a land bill containing the principles adopted in the act upon that subject passed at the last session of Congress.

Resolved, That the governor be requested to transmit copies of the foregoing preamble and resolutions to each of our Senators and Representatives.

It is thus seen that four Senators have declared by their votes that the President, in the late Executive proceedings in relation to the revenue, had been guilty of the impeachable offense of "assuming upon himself authority and power not conferred by the Constitution and laws, but in derogation of both," whilst the legislatures of their respective States had deliberately approved those very proceedings as consistent with the Constitution and demanded by the public good. If these four votes had been given in accordance with the sentiments of the legislatures, as above expressed, there would have been but twenty-two votes out of forty-six for censuring the President, and the unprecedented record of his conviction could not have been placed upon the Journal of the Senate.

In thus referring to the resolutions and instructions of the State legislatures I disclaim and repudiate all authority or design to interfere with the responsibility due from members of the Senate to their own consciences, their constituents, and their country. The facts now stated belong to the history of these proceedings, and are important to the just development of the principles and interests involved in them as well as to the proper vindication of the executive department, and with that view, and that view only, are they here made the topic of remark.

The dangerous tendency of the doctrine which denies to the President the power of supervising, directing, and controlling the Secretary of the Treasury in like manner with the other executive officers would soon be manifest in practice were the doctrine to be established. The President is the direct representative of the American people, but the Secretaries are not. If the Secretary of the Treasury be independent of the President in the execution of the laws, then is there no direct responsibility to the people in that important branch of this Government to which is committed the care of the national finances. And it is in the power of the Bank of the United States, or any other corporation, body of men, or individuals, if a Secretary shall be found to accord with them in opinion or can be induced in practice to promote their views, to control through him the whole action of the Government (so far as it is exercised by his Department) in defiance of the Chief Magistrate elected by the people and responsible to them.

But the evil tendency of the particular doctrine adverted to, though sufficiently serious, would be as nothing in comparison with the pernicious consequences which would inevitably flow from the approbation and allowance by the people and the practice by the Senate of the unconstitutional power of arraigning and censuring the official conduct of the Executive in the manner recently pursued. Such proceedings are eminently calculated to unsettle the foundations of the Government, to disturb the harmonious action of its different departments, and to break down the checks and balances by which the wisdom of its framers sought to insure its stability and usefulness.

The honest differences of opinion which occasionally exist between the Senate and the President in regard to matters in which both are obliged to participate are sufficiently embarrassing. But if the course recently adopted by the Senate shall hereafter be frequently pursued, it is not only obvious that the harmony of the relations between the President and the Senate will be destroyed, but that other and graver effects will ultimately ensue. If the censures of the Senate be submitted to by the President, the confidence of the people in his ability and virtue and the character and usefulness of his administration will soon be at an end, and the real power of the Government will fall into the hands of a body holding their offices for long terms, not elected by the people and not to them directly responsible. If, on the other hand, the illegal censures of the Senate should be resisted by the President, collisions and angry controversies might ensue, discreditable in their progress and in the end compelling the people to adopt the conclusion either that their Chief Magistrate was unworthy of their respect or that the Senate was chargeable with calumny and injustice. Either of these results would impair public confidence in the perfection of the system and lead to serious alterations of its framework or to the practical abandonment of some of its provisions.

The influence of such proceedings on the other departments of the Government, and more especially on the

States, could not fail to be extensively pernicious. When the judges in the last resort of official misconduct themselves overleap the bounds of their authority as prescribed by the Constitution, what general disregard of its provisions might not their example be expected to produce? And who does not perceive that such contempt of the Federal Constitution by one of its most important departments would hold out the strongest temptations to resistance on the part of the State sovereignties whenever they shall suppose their just rights to have been invaded? Thus all the independent departments of the Government, and the States which compose our confederated Union, instead of attending to their appropriate duties and leaving those who may offend to be reclaimed or punished in the manner pointed out in the Constitution, would fall to mutual crimination and recrimination and give to the people confusion and anarchy instead of order and law, until at length some form of aristocratic power would be established on the ruins of the Constitution or the States be broken into separate communities.

Far be it from me to charge or to insinuate that the present Senate of the United States intend in the most distant way to encourage such a result. It is not of their motives or designs, but only of the tendency of their acts, that it is my duty to speak. It is, if possible, to make Senators themselves sensible of the danger which lurks under the precedent set in their resolution, and at any rate to perform my duty as the responsible head of one of the coequal departments of the Government, that I have been compelled to point out the consequences to which the discussion and passage of the resolution may lead if the tendency of the measure be not checked in its inception.

It is due to the high trust with which I have been charged, to those who may be called to succeed me in it, to the representatives of the people whose constitutional prerogative has been unlawfully assumed, to the people and to the States, and to the Constitution they have established that I should not permit its provisions to be broken down by such an attack on the executive department without at least some effort "to preserve, protect, and defend" them. With this view, and for the reasons which have been stated, I do hereby *solemnly protest* against the aforementioned proceedings of the Senate as unauthorized by the Constitution, contrary to its spirit and to several of its express provisions, subversive of that distribution of the powers of government which it has ordained and established, destructive of the checks and safeguards by which those powers were intended on the one hand to be controlled and on the other to be protected, and calculated by their immediate and collateral effects, by their character and tendency, to concentrate in the hands of a body not directly amenable to the people a degree of influence and power dangerous to their liberties and fatal to the Constitution of their choice.

The resolution of the Senate contains an imputation upon my private as well as upon my public character, and as it must stand forever on their journals, I cannot close this substitute for that defense which I have not been allowed to present in the ordinary form without remarking that I have lived in vain if it be necessary to enter into a formal vindication of my character and purposes from such an imputation. In vain do I bear upon my person enduring memorials of that contest in which American liberty was purchased; in vain have I since periled property, fame, and life in defense of the rights and privileges so dearly bought; in vain am I now, without a personal aspiration or the hope of individual advantage, encountering responsibilities and dangers from which by mere inactivity in relation to a single point I might have been exempt, if any serious doubts can be entertained as to the purity of my purposes and motives. If I had been ambitious, I should have sought an alliance with that powerful institution which even now aspires to no divided empire. If I had been venal, I should have sold myself to its designs. Had I preferred personal comfort and official ease to the performance of my arduous duty, I should have ceased to molest it. In the history of conquerors and usurpers, never in the fire of youth nor in the vigor of manhood could I find an attraction to lure me from the path of duty, and now I shall scarcely find an inducement to commence their career of ambition when gray hairs and a decaying frame, instead of inviting to toil and battle, call me to the contemplation of other worlds, where conquerors cease to be honored and usurpers expiate their crimes. The only ambition I can feel is to acquit myself to Him to whom I must soon render an account of my stewardship, to serve my fellow-men, and live respected and honored in the history of my country. No; the ambition which leads me on is an anxious desire and a fixed determination to return to the people unimpaired the sacred trust they have confided to my charge—to heal the wounds of the Constitution and preserve it from further violation; to persuade my countrymen, so far as I may, that it is not in a splendid government supported by powerful monopolies and aristocratical establishments that they will find happiness or their liberties' protection, but in a plain system, void of pomp—protecting all and granting favors to none—dispensing its blessings, like the dews of Heaven, unseen and unfelt save in the freshness and beauty they contribute to produce. It is such a Government that the genius of our people requires—such an one only under which our States may remain for ages to come united, prosperous, and free. If the Almighty Being who has hitherto sustained and protected me will but vouchsafe to make my feeble powers instrumental to such a result, I shall anticipate with pleasure the place to be assigned me in the history of my country, and die contented with the belief that I have contributed in some small degree to increase the value and prolong the duration of American liberty.

To the end that the resolution of the Senate may not be hereafter drawn into precedent with the authority of silent acquiescence on the part of the executive department, and to the end also that my motives and views in the Executive proceedings denounced in that resolution may be known to my fellow-citizens, to the world, and to all posterity, I respectfully request that this message and protest may be entered at length on the journals of the Senate.

Andrew Jackson

April 15th, 1834

VIII · Valedictory

I. "The Counsels of Age and Experience"

ON RETIRING from the Presidency, Jackson, like Washington, could not resist the opportunity to give the American people some final words of advice. Although Jackson's "Farewell Address" lacks the color and militancy that characterize most of his statements on the bank and the Union, it provides a useful summary of his estimate of his major accomplishments as President.

Farewell Address of Andrew Jackson to the People of the United States*

Fellow-Citizens: Being about to retire finally from public life, I beg leave to offer you my grateful thanks for the many proofs of kindness and confidence which I have received at your hands. It has been my fortune, in the discharge of public duties, civil and military, frequently to have found myself in difficult and trying situations where prompt decision and energetic action were necessary and where the interest of the country required that high responsibilities should be fearlessly encountered; and it is with the deepest emotions of gratitude that I acknowledge

* Reprinted from *Register of Debates in Congress,* 24 Congress, 2 Session, House, 1837, XIII, pp. 2165-2177.

the continued and unbroken confidence with which you have sustained me in every trial. My public life has been a long one, and I cannot hope that it has, at all times, been free from errors. But I have the consolation of knowing that, if mistakes have been committed, they have not seriously injured the country I so anxiously endeavored to serve; and, at the moment when I surrender my last public trust, I leave this great people prosperous and happy, in the full enjoyment of liberty and peace, and honored and respected by every nation of the world.

If my humble efforts have in any degree contributed to preserve to you these blessings, I have been more than rewarded by the honors you have heaped upon me and above all, by the generous confidence with which you have supported me in every peril and with which you have continued to animate and cheer my path to the closing hour of my political life. The time has now come when advanced age and a broken frame warn me to retire from public concerns; but the recollection of the many favors you have bestowed upon me is engraven upon my heart, and I have felt that I could not part from your service without making this public acknowledgment of the gratitude I owe you. And if I use the occasion to offer to you the counsels of age and experience, you will, I trust, receive them with the same indulgent kindness which you have so often extended to me; and will, at least, see in them an earnest desire to perpetuate, in this favored land, the blessings of liberty and equal law.

We have now lived almost fifty years under the Constitution framed by the sages and patriots of the Revolution. The conflicts in which the nations of Europe were engaged during a great part of this period, the spirit in which they

waged war against each other, and our intimate commercial connections with every part of the civilized world,
rendered it a time of much difficulty for the Government
of the United States. We have had our seasons of peace
and of war, with all the evils which precede or follow a
state of hostility with powerful nations. We encountered
these trials with our Constitution yet in its infancy, and
under the disadvantages which a new and untried Government must always feel when it is called upon to put
forth its whole strength, without the lights of experience
to guide it or the weight of precedents to justify its measures. But we have passed triumphantly through all these
difficulties. Our Constitution is no longer a doubtful experiment; and, at the end of nearly half a century, we find
that it has preserved unimpaired the liberties of the people, secured the rights of property, and that our country
has improved and is flourishing beyond any former example in the history of nations.

In our domestic concerns there is everything to encourage us, and if you are true to yourselves, nothing can
impede your march to the highest point of national prosperity. The States which had so long been retarded in
their improvement by the Indian tribes residing in the
midst of them are at length relieved from the evil; and this
unhappy race—the original dwellers in our land—are now
placed in a situation where we may well hope that they
will share in the blessings of civilization and be saved
from that degradation and destruction to which they were
rapidly hastening while they remained in the States; and
while the safety and comfort of our own citizens have
been greatly promoted by their removal, the philanthro-
pist will rejoice that the remnant of that ill-fated race has

been at length placed beyond the reach of injury or oppression, and that the paternal care of the General Government will hereafter watch over them and protect them.

If we turn to our relations with foreign Powers, we find our condition equally gratifying. Actuated by the sincere desire to do justice to every nation and to preserve the blessings of peace, our intercourse with them has been conducted on the part of this Government in the spirit of frankness, and I take pleasure in saying that it has generally been met in a corresponding temper. Difficulties of old standing have been surmounted by friendly discussion and the mutual desire to be just; and the claims of our citizens, which had been long withheld, have at length been acknowledged and adjusted, and satisfactory arrangements made for their final payment; and with a limited and, I trust, a temporary exception, our relations with every foreign Power are now of the most friendly character, our commerce continually expanding, and our flag respected in every quarter of the world.

These cheering and grateful prospects and these multiplied favors we owe, under Providence, to the adoption of the Federal Constitution. It is no longer a question whether this great country can remain happily united and flourish under our present form of government. Experience, the unerring test of all human undertakings, has shown the wisdom and foresight of those who formed it; and has proved that in the union of these States there is a sure foundation for the brightest hopes of freedom and for the happiness of the people. At every hazard and by every sacrifice, this Union must be preserved.

The necessity of watching with jealous anxiety for the preservation of the Union was earnestly pressed upon his fellow citizens by the Father of his country in his farewell address. He has there told us that "while experience shall not have demonstrated its impracticability, there will always be reason to distrust the patriotism of those who, in any quarter, may endeavor to weaken its bonds"; and he has cautioned us, in the strongest terms, against the formation of parties on geographical discriminations, as one of the means which might disturb our union, and to which designing men would be likely to resort.

The lessons contained in this invaluable legacy of Washington to his countrymen should be cherished in the heart of every citizen to the latest generation; and, perhaps, at no period of time could they be more usefully remembered than at the present moment. For when we look upon the scenes that are passing around us, and dwell upon the pages of his parting address, his paternal counsels would seem to be not merely the offspring of wisdom and foresight, but the voice of prophecy foretelling events and warning us of the evil to come. Forty years have passed since this imperishable document was given to his countrymen. The Federal Constitution was then regarded by him as an experiment, and he so speaks of it in his address; but an experiment upon the success of which the best hopes of his country depended, and we all know that he was prepared to lay down his life, if necessary, to secure to it a full and a fair trial. The trial has been made. It has succeeded beyond the proudest hopes of those who framed it. Every quarter of this widely extended nation has felt its blessings and shared in the general prosperity produced by its adoption. But amid this general prosperity and splendid success, the dangers of which he warned us are becoming every day more evident and the signs of evil are sufficiently apparent to awaker. the deepest anxiety in the bosom of the patriot. We behold systematic efforts publicly made to sow the seeds of discord between different parts of the United States and to place party divisions directly upon geographical distinctions; to excite the *South* against the *North* and the *North* against the *South,* and to force into the controversy the most delicate and exciting topics—topics upon which it is impossible that a large portion of the Union can ever speak without strong emotion. Appeals, too, are constantly made to sectional interests in order to influence the election of the Chief Magistrate, as if it were desired that he should favor a particular quarter of the country instead of fulfilling the duties of his station with impartial justice to all; and the possible dissolution of the Union has at length become an ordinary and familiar subject of discussion. Has the warning voice of Washington been forgotten? or have designs already been formed to sever the Union? Let it not be supposed that I impute to all of those who have taken an active part in these unwise and unprofitable discussions a want of patriotism or of public virtue. The honorable feeling of State pride and local attachments find a place in the bosoms of the most enlightened and pure. But while such men are conscious of their own integrity and honesty of purpose, they ought never to forget that the citizens of other States are their political brethren; and that, however mistaken they may be in their views, the great body of them are equally honest and upright with themselves. Mutual suspicions and reproaches may in time create mutual hostility, and artful and designing men will always be found who are ready to foment these fatal divisions and to inflame the natural jealousies of different sections of the country. The history of the world is full of such examples and especially the history of republics.

What have you to gain by division and dissension? Delude not yourselves with the belief that a breach once made may be afterwards repaired. If the Union is once severed, the line of separation will grow wider and wider, and the controversies which are now debated and settled in the halls of legislation will then be tried in fields of battle and determined by the sword. Neither should you deceive yourselves with the hope that the first line of separation would be the permanent one, and that nothing but harmony and concord would be found in the new associations formed upon the dissolution of this Union. Local interests would still be found there, and unchastened ambition. And if the recollection of common dangers in which the people of these United States stood side by side against the common foe; the memory of victories won by their united valor; the prosperity and happiness they have enjoyed under the present Constitution; the proud name they bear as citizens of this great republic: if all these recollections and proofs of common interest are not strong enough to bind us together as one people, what tie will hold united the new divisions of empire, when these bonds have been broken and this Union dissevered? The first line of separation would not last for a single generation; new fragments would be torn off; new leaders would spring up; and this great and glorious republic would soon be broken into a multitude of petty states, without commerce, without credit; jealous of one another; armed for mutual aggression; loaded with taxes to pay armies and leaders; seeking aid against each other from foreign powers; insulted and trampled upon by the nations of Europe, until, harassed with conflicts and humbled and debased in spirit, they would be ready to submit to the absolute dominion of any military adventurer and to surrender their liberty for the sake of repose. It is impossible to look on the consequences that would inevitably follow the destruction of this Government and not feel indignant when we hear cold calculations about the value of the Union and have so constantly before us a line of conduct so well calculated to weaken its ties.

There is too much at stake to allow pride or passion to influence your decision. Never for a moment believe that the great body of the citizens of any State or States can deliberately intend to do wrong. They may, under the influence of temporary excitement or misguided opinions, commit mistakes; they may be misled for a time by the suggestions of self-interest; but in a community so enlightened and patriotic as the people of the United States, argument will soon make them sensible of their errors; and, when convinced, they will be ready to repair them. If they have no higher or better motives to govern them, they will at least perceive that their own interest requires them to be just to others as they hope to receive justice at their hands.

But in order to maintain the Union unimpaired, it is absolutely necessary that the laws passed by the constituted authorities should be faithfully executed in every part of the country, and that every good citizen should at all times stand ready to put down with the combined force of the nation every attempt at unlawful resistance under whatever pretext it may be made or whatever shape it may assume. Unconstitutional or oppressive laws may no doubt be passed by Congress, either from erroneous views or the want of due consideration; if they are within the reach of judicial authority, the remedy is easy and peaceful; and if from the character of the law it is an abuse of power not within the control of the judiciary, then free discussion and calm appeals to reason and to the justice of the people will not fail to redress the wrong. But until the law shall be declared void by the courts or repealed by Congress, no individual or combination of individuals can be justified in forcibly resisting its execution. It is impossible that any Government can continue to exist upon any other principles. It would cease to be a Government and be unworthy of the name if it had not the power to enforce the execution of its own laws within its own sphere of action.

It is true that cases may be imagined disclosing such a settled purpose of usurpation and oppression on the part of the Government as would justify an appeal to arms. These, however, are extreme cases, which we have no reason to apprehend in a Government where the power is in the hands of a patriotic people; and no citizen who loves his country would in any case whatever resort to forcible resistance unless he clearly saw that the time had come when a freeman should prefer death to submission; for if such a struggle is once begun and the citizens of one section of the country arrayed in arms against those of another in doubtful conflict, let the battle result as it may, there will be an end of the Union and, with it an end to the hopes of freedom. The victory of the injured would not secure to them the blessings of liberty; it would avenge their wrongs, but they would themselves share in the common ruin.

But the Constitution cannot be maintained nor the Union preserved in opposition to public feeling by the mere exertion of the coercive powers confided to the General Government. The foundations must be laid in the affections of the people; in the security it gives to life, liberty, character, and property, in every quarter of the country; and in the fraternal attachment which the citizens of the several States bear to one another as members of one political family, mutually contributing to promote the happiness of each other. Hence the citizens of every State should studiously avoid everything calculated to wound the sensibility or offend the just pride of the people of other States; and they should frown upon any proceedings within their own borders likely to disturb the tranquillity of their political brethren in other portions of the Union. In a country so extensive as the United States and with pursuits so varied, the internal regulations of the several States must frequently differ from one another in important particulars; and this difference is unavoidably increased by the varying principles upon which the American colonies were originally planted; principles which had taken deep root in their social relations before the Revolution, and, therefore, of necessity influencing their policy since they became free and independent States. But each State has the unquestionable right to regulate its own internal concerns according to its own pleasure; and while it does not interfere with the rights of the people of other States or the rights of the Union, every State must be the sole judge of the measures proper to secure the safety of its citizens and promote their happiness; and all efforts on the part of people of other States to cast odium upon their institutions, and all measures calculated to disturb their rights of property or to put in jeopardy their peace and internal tranquillity are in direct opposition to the spirit in which the Union was formed, and must endanger its safety. Motives of philanthropy may be assigned for this unwarrantable interference; and weak men may persuade themselves for a moment that they are laboring in the cause of humanity and asserting the rights of the human race; but everyone upon sober reflection will see that nothing but mischief can come from these improper assaults upon the feelings and rights of others. Rest assured that the men found busy in this work of discord are not worthy of your confidence and deserve your strongest reprobation.

In the legislation of Congress also and in every measure of the General Government, justice to every portion of the United States should be faithfully observed. No free Government can stand without virtue in the people and a lofty spirit of patriotism; and if the sordid feelings of mere selfishness shall usurp the place which ought to be filled by public spirit, the legislation of Congress will soon be converted into a scramble for personal and sectional advantages. Under our free institutions the citizens of every quarter of our country are capable of attaining a high degree of prosperity and happiness without seeking to profit themselves at the expense of others; and every such attempt must in the end fail to succeed, for the people in every part of the United States are too enlightened not to understand their own rights and interests and to detect and defeat every effort to gain undue advantages over them; and when such designs are discovered, it naturally provokes resentments which cannot always be easily allayed. Justice, full and ample justice, to every portion of the United States should be the ruling principle of every freeman and should guide the deliberations of every public body, whether it be State or national.

It is well known that there have always been those amongst us who wish to enlarge the powers of the General Government; and experience would seem to indicate that there is a tendency on the part of this Government to overstep the boundaries marked out for it by the Constitution. Its legitimate authority is abundantly sufficient for all the purposes for which it was created; and its powers being expressly enumerated, there can be no justification for claiming anything beyond them. Every attempt to exercise power beyond these limits should be promptly and firmly opposed. For one evil example will lead to other measures still more mischievous; and if the principle of constructive powers, or supposed advantages, or temporary circumstances, shall ever be permitted to justify the assumption of a power not given by the Constitution, the General Government will before long absorb all the powers of legislation, and you will have in effect but one consolidated Government. From the extent of our country, its diversified interests, different pursuits, and different habits, it is too obvious for argument that a single consolidated Government would be wholly inadequate to watch over and protect its interests; and every friend of our free institutions should be always prepared to maintain unimpaired and in full vigor the rights and sovereignty of the States and to confine the action of the General Government strictly to the sphere of its appropriate duties.

There is, perhaps, no one of the powers conferred on the Federal Government so liable to abuse as the taxing power. The most productive and convenient sources of revenue were necessarily given to it, that it might be able to perform the important duties imposed upon it; and the taxes which it lays upon commerce being concealed from the real payer in the price of the article, they do not so readily attract the attention of the people as smaller sums demanded from them directly by the tax gatherer. But the tax imposed on goods enhances by so much the price of the commodity to the consumer; and, as many of these duties are imposed on articles of necessity which are daily used by the great body of the people, the money raised by these imposts is drawn from their pockets. Congress has no right, under the Constitution, to take money from the people unless it is required to execute some one of the specific powers intrusted to the Government; and if they raise more than is necessary for such purposes, it is an abuse of the power of taxation and unjust and oppressive. It may, indeed, happen that the revenue will sometimes exceed the amount anticipated when the taxes were laid. When, however, this is ascertained, it is easy to reduce them; and, in such a case, it is unquestionably the duty of the Government to reduce them, for no circumstances can justify it in assuming a power not given to it by the Constitution nor in taking away the money of the people when it is not needed for the legitimate wants of the Government.

Plain as these principles appear to be, you will yet find that there is a constant effort to induce the General Government to go beyond the limits of its taxing power and to impose unnecessary burdens upon the people. Many powerful interests are continually at work to procure heavy duties on commerce and to swell the revenue beyond the real necessities of the public service; and the country has already felt the injurious effects of their combined influence. They succeeded in obtaining a tariff of duties bearing most oppressively on the agricultural and laboring classes of society and producing a revenue that could not be usefully employed within the range of the powers conferred upon Congress; and, in order to fasten upon the people this unjust and unequal system of taxation, extravagant schemes of internal improvement were got up in various quarters to squander the money and to purchase support. Thus, one unconstitutional measure was intended to be upheld by another, and the abuse of the power of taxation was to be maintained by usurping the power of expending the money in internal improvements. You cannot have forgotten the severe and doubtful struggle through which we passed when the Executive Department of the Government, by its veto, endeavored to arrest this prodigal scheme of injustice, and to bring back the legislation of Congress to the boundaries prescribed by the Constitution. The good sense and practical judgment of the people, when the subject was brought before them, sustained the course of the Executive; and this plan of unconstitutional expenditure for the purpose of corrupt influence is, I trust, finally overthrown.

The result of this decision has been felt in the rapid extinguishment of the public debt and the large accumulation of a surplus in the Treasury, notwithstanding the tariff was reduced and is now very far below the amount originally contemplated by its advocates. But, rely upon it, the design to collect an extravagant revenue and to burden you with taxes beyond the economical wants of the Government is not yet abandoned. The various interests which have combined together to impose a heavy tariff

and to produce an overflowing treasury are too strong and
have too much at stake to surrender the contest. The corporations and wealthy individuals who are engaged in
large manufacturing establishments desire a high tariff to
increase their gains. Designing politicians will support it
to conciliate their favor and to obtain the means of profuse
expenditure for the purpose of purchasing influence in
other quarters; and since the people have decided that the
Federal Government cannot be permitted to employ its
income in internal improvements, efforts will be made to
seduce and mislead the citizens of the several States by
holding out to them the deceitful prospect of benefits to
be derived from a surplus revenue collected by the General Government and annually divided among the States.
And if, encouraged by these fallacious hopes, the States
should disregard the principles of economy which ought
to characterize every republican Government and should
indulge in lavish expenditures exceeding their resources,
they will, before long, find themselves oppressed with
debts which they are unable to pay, and the temptation
will become irresistible to support a high tariff in order to
obtain a surplus for distribution. Do not allow yourselves,
my fellow-citizens, to be misled on this subject. The Federal Government cannot collect a surplus for such purposes without violating the principles of the Constitution
and assuming powers which have not been granted. It is,
moreover, a system of injustice, and, if persisted in, will
inevitably lead to corruption and must end in ruin. The
surplus revenue will be drawn from the pockets of the
people, from the farmer, the mechanic, and the laboring
classes of society; but who will receive it when distributed
among the States, where it is to be disposed of by leading

State politicians who have friends to favor and political partisans to gratify? It will certainly not be returned to those who paid it and who have most need of it and are honestly entitled to it. There is but one safe rule, and that is to confine the General Government rigidly within the sphere of its appropriate duties. It has no power to raise a revenue or impose taxes except for the purposes enumerated in the Constitution; and if its income is found to exceed these wants, it should be forthwith reduced, and the burdens of the people so far lightened.

In reviewing the conflicts which have taken place between different interests in the United States and the policy pursued since the adoption of our present form of government, we find nothing that has produced such deep-seated evil as the course of legislation in relation to the currency. The Constitution of the United States unquestionably intended to secure to the people a circulating medium of gold and silver. But the establishment of a national bank by Congress with the privilege of issuing paper money receivable in the payment of the public dues, and the unfortunate course of legislation in the several States upon the same subject, drove from general circulation the constitutional currency and substituted one of paper in its place.

It was not easy for men engaged in the ordinary pursuits of business, whose attention had not been particularly drawn to the subject, to foresee all the consequences of a currency exclusively of paper; and we ought not on that account to be surprised at the facility with which laws were obtained to carry into effect the paper system. Honest and even enlightened men are sometimes misled by the specious and plausible statements of the designing. But experience has now proved the mischiefs and dangers of a paper currency, and it rests with you to determine whether the proper remedy shall be applied.

The paper system being founded on public confidence and having of itself no intrinsic value, it is liable to great and sudden fluctuations, thereby rendering property insecure and the wages of labor unsteady and uncertain. The corporations which create the paper money cannot be relied upon to keep the circulating medium uniform in amount. In times of prosperity, when confidence is high, they are tempted by the prospect of gain, or by the influence of those who hope to profit by it, to extend their issues of paper beyond the bounds of discretion and the reasonable demands of business. And when these issues have been pushed on from day to day until public confidence is at length shaken, then a reaction takes place, and they immediately withdraw the credits they have given; suddenly curtail their issues; and produce an unexpected and ruinous contraction of the circulating medium which is felt by the whole community. The banks by this means save themselves, and the mischievous consequences of their imprudence or cupidity are visited upon the public. Nor does the evil stop here. These ebbs and flows in the currency and these indiscreet extensions of credit naturally engender a spirit of speculation injurious to the habits and character of the people. We have already seen its effects in the wild spirit of speculation in the public lands and various kinds of stock which, within the last year or two, seized upon such a multitude of our citizens and threatened to pervade all classes of society and to withdraw their attention from the sober pursuits of honest industry. It is not by encouraging this spirit that we shall best preserve public virtue and promote the true interests of our country. But if your currency continues as exclusively paper as it now is, it will foster this eager desire to amass wealth without labor; it will multiply the number of dependents on bank accommodations and bank favors; the temptation to obtain money at any sacrifice will become stronger and stronger, and inevitably lead to corruption which will find its way into your public councils and destroy, at no distant day, the purity of your Government. Some of the evils which arise from this system of paper press with peculiar hardship upon the class of society least able to bear it. A portion of this currency frequently becomes depreciated or worthless, and all of it is easily counterfeited in such a manner as to require peculiar skill and much experience to distinguish the counterfeit from the genuine note. These frauds are most generally perpetrated in the smaller notes, which are used in the daily transactions of ordinary business; and the losses occasioned by them are commonly thrown upon the laboring classes of society whose situation and pursuits put it out of their power to guard themselves from these impositions and whose daily wages are necessary for their subsistence. It is the duty of every Government so to regulate its currency as to protect this numerous class as far as practicable from the impositions of avarice and fraud. It is more especially the duty of the United States where the Government is emphatically the Government of the people, and where this respectable portion of our citizens are so proudly distinguished from the laboring classes of all other nations by their independent spirit, their love of liberty, their intelligence, and their high tone of moral character. Their industry in peace is the source of our wealth; and their bravery in war has covered us with glory; and the Government of the United States will but ill discharge its duties if it leaves them a prey to such dishonest impositions. Yet it is evident that their interests cannot be effectually protected unless silver and gold are restored to circulation.

These views alone of the paper currency are sufficient to call for immediate reform; but there is another consideration which should still more strongly press it upon your attention.

Recent events have proved that the paper money system of this country may be used as an engine to undermine your free institutions, and that those who desire to engross all power in the hands of the few and to govern by corruption or force are aware of its power and prepared to employ it. Your banks now furnish your only circulating medium, and money is plenty or scarce according to the quantity of notes issued by them. While they have capitals not greatly disproportioned to each other, they are competitors in business, and no one of them can exercise dominion over the rest; and although, in the present state of the currency, these banks may and do operate injuriously upon the habits of business, the pecuniary concerns, and the moral tone of society; yet, from their number and dispersed situation, they cannot combine for the purpose of political influence; and whatever may be the dispositions of some of them, their power of mischief must necessarily be confined to a narrow space and felt only in their immediate neighborhoods.

But when the charter for the Bank of the United States was obtained from Congress, it perfected the schemes of the paper system and gave to its advocates the position they have struggled to obtain from the commencement of the Federal Government down to the present hour. The immense capital and peculiar privileges bestowed upon it enabled it to exercise despotic sway over the other banks in every part of the country. From its superior strength it could seriously injure, if not destroy, the business of any one of them which might incur its resentment; and it openly claimed for itself the power of regulating the currency throughout the United States. In other words, it asserted (and it undoubtedly possessed) the power to make money plenty or scarce, at its pleasure, at any time, and in any quarter of the Union by controlling the issues of other banks and permitting an expansion or compelling a general contraction of the circulating medium according to its own will. The other banking institutions were sensible of its strength, and they soon generally became its obedient instruments, ready, at all times, to execute its mandates; and with the banks necessarily went, also, that numerous class of persons in our commercial cities who depend altogether on bank credits for their solvency and means of business; and who are, therefore, obliged for their own safety to propitiate the favor of the money power by distinguished zeal and devotion in its service. The result of the ill-advised legislation which established this great monopoly was to concentrate the whole moneyed power of the Union, with its boundless means of corruption and its numerous dependents, under the direction and command of one acknowledged head; thus organizing this particular interest as one body and securing to it unity and concert of action throughout the United States and enabling it to bring forward, upon any occasion, its entire and undivided strength to support or defeat any measure of the Government. In the hands of this formidable power, thus perfectly organized, was also placed unlimited dominion over the amount of the circulating medium, giving it the power to regulate the value of property and the fruits of labor in every quarter of the Union and to bestow prosperity or bring ruin upon any city or section of the country as might best comport with its own interest or policy.

We are not left to conjecture how the moneyed power, thus organized and with such a weapon in its hands, would be likely to use it. The distress and alarm which pervaded and agitated the whole country when the Bank of the United States waged war upon the people in order to compel them to submit to its demands cannot yet be forgotten. The ruthless and unsparing temper with which whole cities and communities were oppressed, individuals impoverished and ruined, and a scene of cheerful prosperity suddenly changed into one of gloom and despondency ought to be indelibly impressed on the memory of the people of the United States. If such was its power in a time of peace, what would it not have been in a season of war with an enemy at your doors? No nation but the freemen of the United States could have come out victorious from such a contest; yet, if you had not conquered, the Government would have passed from the hands of the many to the hands of the few; and this organized money power, from its secret conclave, would have dictated the choice of your highest officers and compelled you to make peace or war as best suited their own wishes. The forms of your government might for a time have remained, but its living spirit would have departed from it.

The distress and sufferings inflicted on the people by

the bank are some of the fruits of that system of policy which is continually striving to enlarge the authority of the Federal Government beyond the limits fixed by the Constitution. The powers enumerated in that instrument do not confer on Congress the right to establish such a corporation as the Bank of the United States; and the evil consequences which followed may warn us of the danger of departing from the true rule of construction and of permitting temporary circumstances or the hope of better promoting the public welfare to influence, in any degree, our decisions upon the extent of the authority of the General Government. Let us abide by the Constitution as it is written or amend it in the constitutional mode if it is found to be defective.

The severe lessons of experience will, I doubt not, be sufficient to prevent Congress from again chartering such a monopoly, even if the Constitution did not present an insuperable objection to it. But you must remember, my fellow citizens, that eternal vigilance by the people is the price of liberty; and that you must pay the price if you wish to secure the blessing. It behooves you, therefore, to be watchful in your States as well as in the Federal Government. The power which the moneyed interest can exercise, when concentrated under a single head, and with our present system of currency, was sufficiently demonstrated in the struggle made by the Bank of the United States. Defeated in the General Government, the same class of intriguers and politicians will now resort to the States and endeavor to obtain there the same organization which they failed to perpetuate in the Union; and with specious and deceitful plans of public advantages and State interests and State pride they will endeavor to es-

tablish in the different States one moneyed institution
with overgrown capital and exclusive privileges sufficient
to enable it to control the operations of the other banks.
Such an institution will be pregnant with the same evils
produced by the Bank of the United States, although its
sphere of action is more confined; and in the State in
which it is chartered the money power will be able to
embody its whole strength and to move together with undivided force to accomplish any object it may wish to
attain. You have already had abundant evidence of its
power to inflict injury upon the agricultural, mechanical,
and laboring classes of society; and over those whose engagements in trade or speculation render them dependent
on bank facilities, the dominion of the State monopoly will
be absolute, and their obedience unlimited. With such a
bank and a paper currency the money power would in a
few years govern the State and control its measures, and
if a sufficient number of States can be induced to create
such establishments, the time will soon come when it will
again take the field against the United States and succeed
in perfecting and perpetuating its organization by a charter from Congress.

It is one of the serious evils of our present system of
banking that it enables one class of society, and that by no
means a numerous one, by its control over the currency
to act injuriously upon the interests of all the others and to
exercise more than its just proportion of influence in political affairs. The agricultural, the mechanical, and the laboring classes have little or no share in the direction of the
great moneyed corporations; and from their habits and
the nature of their pursuits, they are incapable of forming

extensive combinations to act together with united force. Such concert of action may sometimes be produced in a single city or in a small district of country by means of personal communications with each other; but they have no regular or active correspondence with those who are engaged in similar pursuits in distant places; they have but little patronage to give to the press and exercise but a small share of influence over it; they have no crowd of dependents above them who hope to grow rich without labor by their countenance and favor and who are, therefore, always ready to exercise their wishes. The planter, the farmer, the mechanic, and the laborer all know that their success depends upon their own industry and economy and that they must not expect to become suddenly rich by the fruits of their toil. Yet these classes of society form the great body of the people of the United States; they are the bone and sinew of the country; men who love liberty and desire nothing but equal rights and equal laws and who, moreover, hold the great mass of our national wealth, although it is distributed in moderate amounts among the millions of freemen who possess it. But, with overwhelming numbers and wealth on their side, they are in constant danger of losing their fair influence in the Government and with difficulty maintain their just rights against the incessant efforts daily made to encroach upon them. The mischief springs from the power which the moneyed interest derives from a paper currency which they are able to control; from the multitude of corporations with exclusive privileges which they have succeeded in obtaining in the different States and which are employed altogether for their benefit; and unless you become more watchful in your States and check this spirit of monopoly and thirst for exclusive privileges, you will, in the end, find that the most important powers of Government have been given or bartered away, and the control over your dearest interests has passed into the hands of these corporations.

The paper money system and its natural associates—monopoly and exclusive privileges—have already struck their roots deep in the soil; and it will require all your efforts to check its further growth and to eradicate the evil. The men who profit by the abuses and desire to perpetuate them will continue to besiege the halls of legislation in the General Government as well as in the States and will seek, by every artifice, to mislead and deceive the public servants. It is to yourselves that you must look for safety and the means of guarding and perpetuating your free institutions. In your hands is rightfully placed the sovereignty of the country and to you every one placed in authority is ultimately responsible. It is always in your power to see that the wishes of the people are carried into faithful execution, and their will, when once made known, must sooner or later be obeyed. And while the people remain, as I trust they ever will, uncorrupted and incorruptible and continue watchful and jealous of their rights, the Government is safe, and the cause of freedom will continue to triumph over all its enemies.

But it will require steady and persevering exertions on your part to rid yourselves of the iniquities and mischiefs of the paper system and to check the spirit of monopoly and other abuses which have sprung up with it and of which it is the main support. So many interests are united to resist all reform on this subject that you must not hope the conflict will be a short one nor success easy. My humble efforts have not been spared, during my administration of the Government, to restore the constitutional currency of gold and silver; and something, I trust, has been done towards the accomplishment of this most desirable object. But enough yet remains to require all your energy and perseverance. The power, however, is in your hands, and the remedy must and will be applied, if you determine upon it.

While I am thus endeavoring to press upon your attention the principles which I deem of vital importance in the domestic concerns of the country, I ought not to pass over without notice the important considerations which should govern your policy towards foreign Powers. It is, unquestionably, our true interest to cultivate the most friendly understanding with every nation and to avoid by every honorable means the calamities of war; and we shall best attain this object by frankness and sincerity in our foreign intercourse by the prompt and faithful execution of treaties and by justice and impartiality in our conduct to all. But no nation, however desirous of peace, can hope to escape occasional collisions with other Powers; and the soundest dictates of policy require that we should place ourselves in a condition to assert our rights if a resort to force should ever become necessary. Our local situation, our long line of seacoast indented by numerous bays with deep rivers opening into the interior, as well as our extended and still increasing commerce, point to the navy as our natural means of defense. It will, in the end, be found to be the cheapest and most effectual; and now is

the time, in a season of peace, and with an overflowing
revenue, that we can, year after year, add to its strength
without increasing the burdens of the people. It is your
true policy. For your navy will not only protect your rich
and flourishing commerce in distant seas, but will enable
you to reach and annoy the enemy and will give to defense
its greatest efficiency by meeting danger at a distance from
home. It is impossible by any line of fortifications to guard
every point from attack against a hostile force advancing
from the ocean and selecting its object; but they are indispensable to protect cities from bombardment, dock
yards and naval arsenals from destruction; to give shelter
to merchant vessels in time of war, and to single ships or
weaker squadrons when pressed by superior force. Fortifications of this description cannot be too soon completed
and armed and placed in a condition of the most perfect
preparation. The abundant means we now possess cannot
be applied in any manner more useful to the country; and
when this is done and our naval force sufficiently strengthened and our militia armed, we need not fear that any
nation will wantonly insult us or needlessly provoke hostilities. We shall more certainly preserve peace when it
is well understood that we are prepared for war.

In presenting to you, my fellow citizens, these parting
counsels, I have brought before you the leading principles
upon which I endeavored to administer the Government
in the high office with which you twice honored me.
Knowing that the path of freedom is continually beset by
enemies who often assume the disguise of friends, I have
devoted the last hours of my public life to warn you of
the danger. The progress of the United States under our

free and happy institutions has surpassed the most sanguine hopes of the founders of the Republic. Our growth has been rapid beyond all former example, in numbers, in wealth, in knowledge, and all the useful arts which contribute to the comforts and convenience of man; and from the earliest ages of history to the present day, there never have been thirteen millions of people associated together in one political body who enjoyed so much freedom and happiness as the people of these United States. You have no longer any cause to fear danger from abroad; your strength and power are well known throughout the civilized world, as well as the high and gallant bearing of your sons. It is from within, among yourselves, from cupidity, from corruption, from disappointed ambition, and inordinate thirst for power, that factions will be formed and liberty endangered. It is against such designs, whatever disguise the actors may assume, that you have especially to guard yourselves. You have the highest of human trusts committed to your care. Providence has showered on this favored land blessings without number and has chosen you as the guardians of freedom to preserve it for the benefit of the human race. May He who holds in his hands the destinies of nations make you worthy of the favors He has bestowed and enable you, with pure hearts and pure hands and sleepless vigilance, to guard and defend to the end of time the great charge he has committed to your keeping.

My own race is nearly run; advanced age and failing health warn me that before long I must pass beyond the reach of human events and cease to feel the vicissitudes of human affairs. I thank God that my life has been spent in a land of liberty and that He has given me a heart to love my country with the affection of a son. And, filled with gratitude for your constant and unwavering kindness, I bid you a last and affectionate farewell.

Andrew Jackson

March 4, 1837

SUGGESTED READINGS ON ANDREW JACKSON
AND JACKSONIAN DEMOCRACY

SUGGESTED READINGS ON ANDREW JACKSON
AND JACKSONIAN DEMOCRACY

Abernethy, Thomas Perkins, *From Frontier to Plantation in Tennessee.* Chapel Hill: University of North Carolina Press, 1932.

Bassett, John Spencer, ed., *Correspondence of Andrew Jackson,* seven vols. Washington: Carnegie Institution, 1926-1935.

Bassett, John Spencer, *Life of Andrew Jackson,* two vols. in one. New York: The Macmillan Company, 1931.

Blau, Joseph Leon, ed., *Social Theories of Jacksonian Democracy.* New York: Hafner Publishing Company, Inc., 1947.

Boucher, Chauncey S., *The Nullification Controversy in South Carolina.* Chicago: University of Chicago Press, 1916.

Bowers, Claude G., *Party Battles of the Jackson Period.* Boston: Houghton Mifflin Company, 1922.

Catterall, Ralph Charles H., *The Second Bank of the United States.* Chicago: University of Chicago Press, 1903.

Gammon, Samuel Rhea, Jr., *The Presidential Campaign of 1832.* Baltimore: Johns Hopkins Press, 1922.

Grace Madeleine, Sister, *Monetary and Banking Theories of Jacksonian Democracy.* Philadelphia: University of Pennsylvania Press, 1943.

Heiskell, Samuel G., *Andrew Jackson and Early Tennessee History.* Nashville: Ambrose printing company, 1920-1921.

James, Marquis, *Andrew Jackson: The Border Captain.* Indianapolis: The Bobbs-Merrill Company, Inc., 1933.

James, Marquis, *Andrew Jackson: Portrait of a President.* Indianapolis: The Bobbs-Merrill Company, Inc., 1937.

Parton, James, *Life of Andrew Jackson,* three vols. New York: D. Appleton Co., 1860.

Schlesinger, Arthur M., Jr., *The Age of Jackson.* Boston: Little Brown & Co., 1945.

Sumner, William Graham, *Andrew Jackson as a Public Man.* Boston: Houghton Mifflin Company, 1882.

Turner, Frederick J., *The United States, 1830-1850.* New York: Henry Holt & Co., 1935.

Wiltse, Charles M., *John C. Calhoun, Nullifier, 1829-1839.* Indianapolis: The Bobbs-Merrill Company, Inc., 1949.

INDEX

INDEX

A

Adams, John, 93
Adams, John Quincy, 24, 25, 81, 88-90
Albany Regency, 25
Ambrister, Robert C., 72
American economy during Jackson's lifetime, 40
American Revolution, Jackson's part in, 55-58
Apalachicola ("Appelachecola") River, 70
Arbuthnot, Alexander, 72
Aristocracy on Tennessee frontier, 22
Articles of Confederation, Jackson's comments on, 109-110

B

Banking, *see* Second Bank of the United States
Banks, state, 29; Jackson's views on, 174-175, 201-204
Benton, Thomas Hart, 32
Biddle, Nicholas, 26

C

Calhoun, John C., 27, 133; and Eaton affair, 34; views on the nature of the Union, 35-38
Camden, South Carolina, 55
Campbell, George W., letter to, concerning the Florida expedition, 70-75
Civil service, *see* Spoils system
Class distinctions, Jackson's attitude toward, 23, 44-45
Clay, Henry, 24, 26-27, 84-90, 133
Coffee, John, 64
Coleman, L. H., letter to, concerning the tariff, 78-81
Compromise Tariff, 37, 132
Constitution, Jackson's views on, 26, 29, 109-132, 137-154, 169-172, 205, 207-208, 216-257, 262, 268
"Corrupt bargain," 24; Jackson's views on, 88-90
Crawford, Andrew J., letter to, concerning the end of the nullification controversy, 133-134